Praise for *8 Great Smarts for Homeschoolers*

Mrs. Hollenbeck helps parents identify their children's multiple intelligence strengths and then gives practical suggestions for how each major subject can be adapted to those styles. As the author of many science courses for homeschooling, I really appreciated her discussion of the various ways science can be personalized to meet the needs of each child as well as her approach to lab reports. More importantly, she emphasizes over and over again that each child is a unique masterpiece made by God. Whether you are a new homeschooling parent or a veteran homeschooler, you will benefit from reading *8 Great Smarts for Homeschoolers*.

JAY L. WILE, author of Science Through History and the Discovering Design series

For too long, homeschool moms have tried to make their children fit a standard education. It works with some, but for others, it can have disastrous results accompanied by tears and guilt. Tina Hollenbeck's book *8 Great Smarts for Homeschoolers* shows you how to tailor education to fit the individual child . . . more specifically, YOUR child. Tina walks you step-by-step through the main areas of study and shows you how to use the eight great smarts to maximize your child's learning . . . giving you a child who smiles again.

TODD WILSON, founder, The Smiling Homeschooler, The Familyman

8 Great Smarts for Homeschoolers is a revolutionary guide for raising confident kids who love to learn. Capturing the very essence of home education, Tina Hollenbeck shows parents how to help children embrace and excel in their God-given interests and abilities. I wish I would have had this book during our homeschooling years.

GINGER HUBBARD, bestselling author of *Don't Make Me Count to Three* and *I Can't Believe You Just Said That*; cohost of the podcast *Parenting with Ginger Hubbard*

As a homeschooling mom of ten children, I thought I'd "learned" all I could about teaching them. After all, I've been homeschooling for over twenty-five years. How wrong I was! *8 Great Smarts for Homeschoolers* is insightful, helpful, and encouraging. It's filled with wonderful insights on how to activate my kids' smarts. I'm excited about helping my kids explore content in new ways to discover how truly brilliant they are! And I can't wait to share this resource with friends.

TRICIA GOYER, homeschooling mom an~~d~~ *Grumble Free Year*

I have successfully used the eight smarts popularized by Dr. Kathy Koch when homeschooling my youngest children. Because Tina Hollenbeck lists many teaching ideas for each smart by academic area, it will now be even easier. If you want to become a better teacher and avoid the frustration that comes from the useless "slower and louder" method, this book is for you! You'll learn exactly how to use a different smart when reteaching concepts—and find success for your child and yourself. I'm grateful for this resource!

HEIDI ST. JOHN, author of *Becoming MomStrong*, host of the Heidi St. John podcast, founder of MomStrongInternational.com, and candidate for Congress in Washington's 3rd congressional district

Filled with helpful suggestions and educational strategies, this book walks parents through teaching the various school subjects through the lens of their children's unique giftedness—their smarts. It goes beyond being a curriculum guide, encouraging parents in their God-given position of pouring into their children: awakening and strengthening smarts, learning with them, and loving them.

SHERRI SELIGSON, international speaker, marine biologist, author, and veteran homeschool mom

For most homeschool parents, relationships with their children are paramount. Many worry, though, that academics will get in the way of that, putting a strain on the parent/child relationship by wedging the role of teacher into the mix. In *8 Great Smarts for Homeschoolers*, Tina Hollenbeck does a wonderful job of helping parents better understand their children. Tina opens a whole new world of thinking for homeschooling families, teaching them how their children's natural strengths and bents can best be approached as they teach each subject. The insight she offers is sure to be an encouragement and help to homeschool parents just starting out or at any point in their journey.

LESLIE NUNNERY, cofounder of Teach Them Diligently and the author of *Teach Them Diligently: Raising Children of Promise*

There is perhaps no greater hurdle for homeschool parents than letting go of the damaging idea of standardized education. Tina highlights not only the importance of knowing the different ways that our children excel, but she also shows the reader how we can apply that knowledge to key subject areas. By developing the unique gifts and smarts of our children, we enable them to soar as the individuals that God created to be.

TARA BENTLEY, Executive Director, Indiana Association of Home Educators

In *8 Great Smarts for Homeschoolers*, Tina Hollenbeck gives practical ideas about how to best teach every subject using our children's innate intelligences—I've never seen anything like it. Finally, a simple, comprehensive roadmap that ditches arbitrary school "norms" and shows us how to work with—instead of against—our children's unique smarts. It's a game-changer that will save time, frustration, tears, and lots of money when choosing methods, assignments, and curriculum to help our children reach their full potential.

ANNE MILLER, president and executive director of Home Educators Association of Virginia and the recipient of the Chris Klicka Award for courage and commitment to serving homeschool families for 35 years

In her new book, *8 Great Smarts for Homeschoolers*, Tina Hollenbeck shows how you can use the freedom and flexibility of homeschooling to customize your children's education around their unique gifts. Ideas and examples for teaching all the school subjects at home in ways that fit well with each of the eight intelligences make this a helpful, practical resource. This short and interesting book could very well transform your homeschool experience.

REBECCA LIAO, Chief Customer Officer, Teaching Textbooks

A great practical guide for new and seasoned homeschoolers alike, *8 Great Smarts for Homeschoolers* will give you invaluable tools to discern the individual needs and the learning styles of your own children. Here is simple, direct, and easy-to-understand information you will refer to over and over again. Tina will become a kind friend as you walk through the pages of her book. This is a resource you don't want to be without as you navigate the wonderful world of homeschooling!

KAREN CAMPBELL, author of *The Joy of Relationship Homeschooling: When the One Anothers Come Home*

8 Great Smarts for Homeschoolers is the book that will help transform your desire to create a tailor-made education for your kids into actionable steps. Using Dr. Kathy Koch's *8 Great Smarts* as a guide, Tina Hollenbeck has assembled a valuable toolbox of homeschool resources and ideas that will show you how to tap into the natural learning strengths of each of your children, ensuring that they'll have a more meaningful and engaging education.

JAMIE ERICKSON, author of *Homeschool Bravely* and cohost of the *Mom to Mom Podcast*

To say this book is an invaluable tool for homeschooling parents would be an understatement. Each page is filled with practical, essential information that every homeschooling family *needs*. As a veteran homeschooling mom of eight kids, I encourage parents to be students of their children because it's one of the most effective ways to gather the information we need to customize their education. I encourage every homeschooling parent to dive into this incredibly helpful book. You're going to love it!

DURENDA WILSON, author of *The Four Hour School Day* and *The Unhurried Homeschooler* and host of *The Durenda Wilson Podcast*

Rather than feeling "less than" during academic studies, children who recognize that their smarts ARE smart will find powerful new ways of navigating, even enjoying, subjects that have been difficult in the past. Dr. Kathy Koch, in her excellent book, *8 Great Smarts*, provided the homeschool community with tremendous insight, knowledge, and encouragement about these smarts. Now, Tina Hollenbeck's new book adds another layer of usability for homeschooling families as she shares practical (and wonderful) ways of integrating these smarts into every subject area. I'm excited for new doors to open for parents and children through this book, and for more children to experience the JOY of learning in ways that honor their unique design.

DIANA WARING, pioneer homeschooler and author of the History Revealed curriculum, the Experience History Through Music series, and the new Yearning to Breathe Free American history curriculum

As a word smart / people smart individual, I love the study of personality types. Imagine my joy to discover that Tina Hollenbeck (a friend and gifted writer) teamed up with Kathy Koch to apply the *8 Great Smarts* to homeschool! As a retired homeschool mom, I'm applying these truths to my word smart / nature smart grandchildren—with inspiring walks and talks in the woods! This resource is a gift for all those seeking to encourage children in their God-given abilities.

LINDA LACOUR HOBAR, author of *The Mystery of History*

8 Great Smarts for Homeschoolers by Tina Hollenbeck is an informative book every homeschool parent should have on their bookshelf. Hollenbeck skillfully uses practical examples to illustrate how each of the *8 Great Smarts* by Koch applies to teaching children at home.

CONNIE ALBERS, author of *Parenting Beyond the Rules*, founder of *Equipped To Be* podcast, homeschool veteran of five

8 GREAT SMARTS
FOR HOME
SCHOOLERS

A Guide to Teaching Based on Your Child's Unique Strengths

TINA HOLLENBECK

MOODY PUBLISHERS
CHICAGO

Edited by Annette LaPlaca
Interior Design: Puckett Smartt
Cover Design: Kaylee Lockenour
Cover image of brain icon copyright © 2015 by Daniel Rodríguez Quintana/Stocksy (69957685). All rights reserved.

All websites and phone numbers listed herein are accurate at the time of publication but may change in the future or cease to exist. The listing of website references and resources does not imply publisher endorsement of the site's entire contents. Groups and organizations are listed for informational purposes, and listing does not imply publisher endorsement of their activities.

Library of Congress Cataloging-in-Publication Data
Names: Hollenbeck, Tina, author.
Title: 8 great smarts for homeschoolers : a guide to teaching based on your
    child's unique strengths / Tina Hollenbeck.
Other titles: Eight great smarts for homeschoolers
Description: Chicago : Moody Publishers, [2021] | Includes bibliographical
    references. | Summary: "A Christian counseling model can't just be about
    admonishment. That approach only leads to shame and human efforts that
    are doomed to fail. But when the gospel is brought to bear in the
    counseling relationship, the counselor becomes an instrument of grace in
    the hands of a faithful God"-- Provided by publisher.
Identifiers: LCCN 2021013986 (print) | LCCN 2021013987 (ebook) | ISBN
    9780802423238 (paperback) | ISBN 9780802499547 (ebook)
Subjects: LCSH: Home schooling--Religious aspects--Christianity. |
    Counseling--Religious aspects--Christianity. | Pastoral counseling. |
    BISAC: RELIGION / Christian Ministry / Counseling & Recovery
Classification: LCC LC40 .H823 2021 (print) | LCC LC40 (ebook) | DDC
    371.04/2--dc23
LC record available at https://lccn.loc.gov/2021013986
LC ebook record available at https://lccn.loc.gov/2021013987

Originally delivered by fleets of horse-drawn wagons, the affordable paperbacks from D. L. Moody's publishing house resourced the church and served everyday people. Now, after more than 125 years of publishing and ministry, Moody Publishers' mission remains the same—even if our delivery systems have changed a bit. For more information on other books (and resources) created from a biblical perspective, go to www.moodypublishers.com or write to:

Moody Publishers
820 N. LaSalle Boulevard
Chicago, IL 60610

1 3 5 7 9 10 8 6 4 2

Printed in the United States of America

For Jeff, Rachel, and Abbie.
Thank you, Jeff, for trusting me as the
primary educator of our precious girls,
and for everything you've done to facilitate me
being home with them.
Abbie and Rachel, being your mom is my greatest joy.
I am humbled beyond measure that the Lord
entrusted you to me;
I hope you always know my love for you
is unconditional and eternal.

CONTENTS

FOREWORD:

Because You Teach
CHILDREN

When I taught second graders, I was saddened by the number of my students who already thought of themselves as incapable or stupid. I was not only sad for them, I was also concerned for my role as their teacher. Would I be able to teach them if they doubted themselves?

I didn't learn about Howard Gardner's discovery that we have the capacity to develop eight different smarts until after I earned my PhD and began teaching at the University of Wisconsin–Green Bay. I loved inspiring my students, who were training to become teachers, to teach their future students according to *how* they were smart. This is where I met Tina Hollenbeck. She was one of the best thinkers and writers I taught, so the publication of her work is exciting.

When I taught the eight smarts to Tina and other students, I remembered my Leslie, Rafe, Jessica, Brian, and so many others from years before. Maybe this is why Rafe loved science when we studied magnets but didn't when we studied fruit flies. He was more *logic smart* than *nature smart.* It was why Leslie lacked self-control on days she had art. She was *picture smart.* This was why Jessica begged to participate in groups and others didn't. She was *people smart.* And I believe Brian's desire to draw the shape of words he was learning and post them on the wall was because he was *picture smart, nature smart,* and *body smart.*

Because you've answered the call to homeschool, you'll truly know your children. You'll be with them—a lot! It may feel constant. It will be constant some days or even weeks. This is beautiful. This is family! Your relationship will be strengthened, and you'll be empowered to make the difference that you hope to make in their todays and tomorrows.

Tina will help you discover that your children are smart in eight different ways. Their smarts will explain a lot: why you might enjoy spending time with one of your children more than another, why one child beats you playing chess while the other doesn't enjoy the game at all, why one is motivated by worship while another isn't, and more.

As a homeschooling parent, your major takeaways will be

about teaching and learning. Through Tina's explanations and examples, you'll learn what topics each child will be most interested in, what teaching and curricula styles may work best, and what learning methods to employ. You will be encouraged as she provides you with the foundation and supporting beams that allow you to design an educational program that works.

When I teach at homeschool conventions, I regularly say, "You teach children; you don't teach math, reading, or Bible. Teaching them how to learn and to love learning will make them the leaders you want them to be." Understanding the eight great smarts will help you accomplish these goals. I pray you successfully implement Tina's ideas and enjoy the journey.

KATHY KOCH, PHD
Founder, Celebrate Kids, Inc.

From Where Did I COME, and Where Are We GOING?

I met Kathy Koch in the mid-1980s, when I was a student at the university where she taught. When I began my teacher-training studies, I took two of Kathy's classes and also got to know her through church and as the advisor of our campus InterVarsity Christian Fellowship chapter. She became a Titus 2 woman in my life and stood up in my wedding. Over time, she and I got into the habit of meeting regularly for walk-and-talks, during which she listened and counseled as I worked through some difficult personal struggles, and I listened and encouraged as she spoke of her dream to move on from the university and launch Celebrate Kids.

We maintained and grew our friendship when she relocated a thousand miles away to make her dream come true. This was back in the days of dial-up—when, if you can believe it, we couldn't use the internet if the home phone was already in use. I remember well my husband, Jeff, scrawling little notes to me as I chatted—for hours—with Kathy: *Will you be done soon? It's been three hours and I really need the computer so I can use the internet.*

Fast-forward several years to 2001 and 2002, when the Lord blessed Jeff and me with the two greatest joys of our lives: our Irish-twin daughters, Rachel and Abbie. We had waited so long to have them because of my concerns that I wouldn't be a good enough mother. But God had used Kathy and others to cover—and eventually replace—my anxiety with faith. And then the instruction and encouragement Kathy provided to parents all across America and in many other countries became real in my life as well.

Of all the wisdom and insight Kathy provided to me over the years, the message delivered in *8 Great Smarts* probably had the greatest impact on a practical level. She had taught about "the smarts" at the university, and I'd applied as much of the theory as I could during my nine years as a public-school teacher. And when I came home to raise my babies, Kathy was in the midst of birthing her writing career, knowing that the content in what became *Five to Thrive* and *8 Great Smarts* would be her first two "literary babies."[1] Thus, the early years of my parenting adventure were bathed—via long phone conversations as she hammered out those books—in the theory of multiple intelligences and how to apply it to kids' lives.

I had developed an interest in homeschooling long before the girls were born, when I was privileged as a newlywed to meet a couple of "modern pioneer" homeschooling moms at church. My stint teaching in public schools—though successful—confirmed my desire. Jeff wasn't sure. He had some of the common questions and concerns—i.e., what would his family think, would our kids seem "weird" to others, could they go to college—but when he met several homeschooled teens while serving as the interim youth pastor at church, the die was cast. He described the intellectual curiosity and ease with which the homeschooled kids consistently interacted—with him and the other leaders, as well as with all the other kids in the group—and said, "If that's what homeschooling does, I'm in."

We concluded that homeschooling was God's call and conviction for our family, and we never looked back.[2] We committed to homeschooling all the way through to high school graduation, and ideas and principles from the first version of *8 Great Smarts* became an integral part of our approach.

Because I knew the model from before Abbie and Rachel were old enough to demonstrate an affinity for any particular smarts, I understood that I should expose them to resources and activities that would activate all the smarts.[3] I also kept a lookout in due time for evidence of which were the top smarts for each of the girls, and I was conscious of trying to avoid paralyzing any developing strengths.[4] I used my knowledge of the girls' smarts profiles when choosing curriculum—and when deciding that formal curriculum wasn't always necessary. Then, when one or the other of the girls hit an academic wall, I referred to my understanding of the smarts in seeking a solution or work-around.

Time raced on, and my daughters became adults in what seemed like the blink of an eye. We graduated them (together) from our homeschool in June 2020. And, though their adult lives have only just begun, I see enough from the trajectory on which each is currently traveling to believe that our homeschool venture—with all its inevitable ups and downs and twists and turns—has landed them both in a good place from which to begin the next phase of their respective journeys.

Every smart is equally important and valuable.

But what about you? Maybe you have little ones you're planning to homeschool in a few years. Maybe you've been educating your kids at home for years and wonder if you've blown it because you've only just now heard about the smarts—and you're not quite sure what they actually are. Or maybe you have school-aged kids or teens you've recently pulled from a conventional public or private school, hoping against hope you don't screw 'em up!

First, understand that you can't wreck your kids by homeschooling—nor by just recently learning about the smarts. Second, realize that learning about multiple intelligences (i.e., "the smarts") will not give you the perfect homeschool; there is no such thing as a perfect home, perfect kids, or perfect parents, so you can drop that notion right now.[5] But knowledge of the smarts and how to apply them to your home learning program is good gear for your parenting toolbox—"gadgets," so to speak, that will increase your peace and confidence as a homeschooler and bless your kids, now and for the long-haul.

As you consider wielding these smarts tools, let me recommend actually reading *8 Great Smarts* if you haven't already.[6] My goal is to get you thinking about applications of the theory to homeschooling, and that will make more sense if you've already pondered Kathy's detailed analysis and engaging examples and analogies.

Homeschooling provides the freedom and opportunity to help our kids explore and develop all eight smarts to their highest potential.

But if you're dying to jump right in to implementing relevant ideas in your home, let me provide you with a working smarts vocabulary to get you going, taken directly from *8 Great Smarts*. Please understand that this list is not a hierarchy; in fact, though word and logic smart are prioritized within institutional school settings, every smart is equally important and valuable. Indeed, the customized nature of homeschooling provides us with the freedom and opportunity to help our kids explore and develop all eight to their highest potential.

- **Word Smart** people think with words. When excited, they talk and might write. Children who are particularly smart in this area can argue, persuade, entertain, and/or instruct effectively through the spoken word. They tend to be masters of literacy: they read a lot, write clearly, listen intently, and/or speak well.

- **Logic Smart** people think with questions. When excited, they ask more questions. Logically inclined children have the ability to reason, sequence, categorize, and think in terms of cause-effect and comparison-contrast relationships.

- **Picture Smart** people think with their eyes and with pictures. When excited, they add to their pictures (in their minds and on paper). Children who are picture smart are very sensitive to visual details. They have the ability to observe, transform, and re-create different aspects of the visual-spatial world.

- **Music Smart** people think with rhythms and melodies. When excited, they make music. Musically gifted children are able to hear, appreciate, and/or produce rhythms and melodies. They often have a good ear, can sing in tune, keep time to music, and listen to different musical selections with some degree of discernment.

- **Body Smart** people think with movement and touch. When excited, they move more. Evidence of body intelligence is seen via strong large motor and/or small motor skills and interests. These children are talented in controlling their body movements and/or in handling objects skillfully. They may enjoy physical pursuits like walking, sports, dancing, acting, or camping and/or they may be skilled at activities like sewing, carpentry, or model-building.

• **Nature Smart** people think with patterns. When excited, they go outside. Children who would rather be outdoors than indoors may be strong in this smart. They tend to love animals and are knowledgeable about them. They also are skilled at recognizing and classifying plants, minerals, and animals. The ability to categorize cultural artifacts like cars or sneakers may also depend on this smart.

• **People Smart** people think with other people. When excited, they talk to people. Children with this intelligence are able to discern and then respond to the moods, intentions, and desires of others. Therefore, they tend to be leaders. They have the ability (for good or bad) to get inside another person and view the world from that individual's perspective.

• **Self Smart** people think with deep reflection. When excited, they spend time alone thinking. Children strong in this smart can use their self-understanding to enrich and guide their lives. They tend to enjoy quiet times of deep soul-searching. They also need peace, space, privacy, and quiet. They are fiercely independent, highly goal-directed, and intensely self-disciplined.

Even though homeschooling is about so much more than academic content—in fact, home-based learning is a holistic lifestyle that reaches into every facet of family life—it's a common cultural norm to organize our thinking about "school," including home-based school, according to various "subject areas." Thus, I might ask my friend what curriculum she's using for math this year, or the new homeschooler with whom I'm having coffee may wonder about my favorite world-history resource.

Addressing subject areas to suit children's unique smarts profiles is one of the greatest gifts we can give—right now and for their long-term happiness and success.

With that framework in mind, I've organized the following discussion by broad subject area—math, language arts, science, social studies, fine arts, electives, and religious education—in order to share ideas about how to awaken, strengthen, and utilize each of the smarts to help your children learn and master the various sorts of academic content. Indeed, one of the many beautiful features of homeschooling is an ability to customize instruction according to how each child has been intrinsically wired. So addressing different subject areas in ways that suit children's unique smarts profiles is one of the greatest gifts we can give—right now and for their long-term happiness and success.

I'm not about the business of endorsing particular curricula, either here or on my comprehensive online database, The Homeschool Resource Roadmap,[7] because I believe you can best discern which material might ultimately work well for each of your children. Many good products exist, and I will mention some that have stood out to me as exemplars illustrating specific points. But it's your privilege to find what ultimately suits your kids.

The products and books I will reference can all be checked out using the internet. But I hope The Roadmap, and perhaps even my Route-Finder tool,[8] can be of help as well. To that end, you might want to visit and bookmark The Roadmap, where all the resources mentioned—and so many more!—are listed, charted, and hyperlinked right back to company websites.[9]

I hope the next seven chapters bless your socks off. But in my view, the last chapter is the most important (don't look now; save the best till last!) because it describes the bedrock foundation that underpins and supports the daily comings and goings of any healthy homeschool. Without that foundation, the various rooms (subjects)—no matter how beautifully decorated—will easily crumble at the slightest (inevitable) provocation. It's imperative that we build and maintain the foundation at all times.

MATH:

From Here to
INFINITY

When my daughters were about four and five, I was working with them on counting. Abbie could pretty easily count as high as requested, but Rachel struggled to get past twenty. No matter how I coaxed or cajoled, she simply couldn't remember and consistently apply the counting pattern.

One day in the midst of my trying to figure out how to help her, she came to the dining room for her "math lesson" as requested. I was jotting a note in my planner, so Rachel began skipping around the table. That didn't faze me, as she was a very active child. What did get my attention, though, was her counting. As she skipped, she counted. She got to twenty—and kept going. Higher and higher she counted—all the way to a hundred before stopping and plopping down to do math. My mouth wasn't exactly hanging open, but it might as well have been.

"Rachel," I asked, "can you do that again?"

Still sitting down, she smiled and started. Right around twenty, though, she paused, frowned, and stopped. "I can't remember more."

"That's okay, hon. What about trying it again as you skip around the table?"

She jumped up. "Really?!" It wasn't every day—or any day—that math happened in motion.

She began skipping and counting, reciting the numbers in her airy, sing-song voice until she once again reached a hundred. Then she stopped, happy as a clam, and asked, "Is that enough, Momma?"

Over the next few days, I experimented with her, asking her to count while sitting and then again while moving in some way.

It's imperative to understand and embrace the truth that our kids will not be good at everything.

Every single time she was still, she struggled. Each time she was in motion, she could keep going as long as I let her.

It had already dawned on me that Rachel was body smart. Though it was really too early in her life to pinpoint her smarts strengths, I was quite certain—based on her confidence and grace when in motion—that she was. I had an inkling that music smart might be strong for her as well.

By skipping or hopping or jogging while chanting numbers in time to her stride, Rachel was activating both smarts to accomplish a learning task. When she was sitting still and counting, the rhythm didn't kick in, leaving her doubly hamstrung.

In the spirit of full disclosure, I must admit that Rachel never grew to like math and would, in fact, call herself a math struggler. She worked hard to master the typical arithmetic functions so she's competent with the math most people use throughout their lives, and she managed geometry because of her picture- and body-smart strengths. But algebra completely befuddled her. And we realized that God has wired her such that she doesn't need to master "higher math" in order to live a happy, successful adult life.

I believe it's imperative to understand and embrace the truth that our kids will not be good at everything—because no human being on the planet is wired to master the full, complete scope of human knowledge and skill. In reality—no matter what curriculum we buy or which methods we employ (even when we match instruction to a child's multiple intelligence strengths)—some kids simply will not soar in math. Others will always struggle with writing or science or art. In order to help each child actually maximize her own *real* potential, we must decide to be okay with that. As Kathy says almost every time she speaks, "Raise the child you have, not the one you wish you had."

That doesn't mean we don't try—and expect the child to try.

Laziness should never be an option. Nor does it mean leaving a child ignorant of an area of study she really must master to be a productive member of society. But we can set customized, realistic goals for each child based on our best understanding of what each will *actually* need to launch well into adult life as a unique individual, without feeling trapped by some idea of what "everyone else" does. Some kids do need four (or more) credits of higher math on a transcript, but many do not. Many people obtain a four-year college degree without studying calculus.[1]

And whatever level of math your uniquely designed child should strive to attain, there are ways she can use her smarts to get there.

Logic Smart

God has gifted some children with what seems to be a natural affinity for math. Nathan, the eldest son of my friends Ron and Wendy, is a good example. Nathan is bright in general, but he grasps even the trickiest mathematical concepts almost as easily as he breathes. He became a National Merit Scholar based largely on his mathematical acuity and, after earning a double major in mechanical engineering and applied math, considered earning a PhD in engineering before following God's call into ministry. Nathan—like many who excel in math—has a high degree of logic smart. Likewise, if your child has a strong ability to reason, sequence, and categorize, math may appear to come naturally to her. She may still need some guidance and motivation, but logic-smart kids are most likely to become self-directed in their math studies and are able to master advanced content with relative ease.

Body Smart

You've read how I discovered quite by accident that being able to move helped Rachel remember and apply number facts. This idea seems strange at first glance, as most of us grew up attending institutional schools, where sitting still in neat rows of desks was a virtue. But most young children of about age ten and younger are intrinsically wired to move a lot. And that's even more true of kids who are body smart. So there is nothing wrong—and much right—with devising ways to use movement to facilitate math instruction.

In addition to skipping or hopping while counting or reciting math facts, you can also incorporate calisthenics. Can you picture a child doing jumping jacks or burpees while reviewing the multiplication tables or a teen running through theorems in the midst of a Pilates routine? And in the true spirit of homeschool multitasking, such activity can double as physical education time!

Don't let it annoy you if a child taps her pencil or jiggles her leg while studying; just teach her to tap on a quiet surface, such as her leg, so as not to disturb her siblings. Additionally, consider purchasing an exercise ball on which the child can sit while working through math assignments. This seems counterintuitive, as if the movement would cause distraction. But for body-smart kids, movement activates concentration.

Encourage the use of Unifix Cubes, an abacus, and even a child's own fingers. For a body-smart child of any age, manipulatives are not cheating; they're legitimate learning tools. Body-smart kids make neurological connections through movement, so the more often they can manipulate objects while attempting to learn concepts, the more likely the ideas are to "stick." Curricula that employ a Montessori, Waldorf, or Project-Based approach will likely resonate with a body-smart child.

Nature Smart

In some ways, nature smart complements both logic and body smart. Those with a high degree of nature smart enjoy classifying and categorizing like those with logic smart, and their pleasure at being outside usually comes with an interest in moving in some way—whether via gross-motor skills such as walking, climbing, or jogging, or fine-motor activity that accompanies searching for and collecting various natural specimens. We can use this to a child's advantage when learning math.

For example, instead of buying plastic manipulatives, use the rocks, leaves, and sticks a nature-smart child is apt to gather as counting and arithmetic tools. And, as you're out on nature walks hunting for treasures, help the child to discover the mathematical beauty that God has built into Creation—i.e., how the design on every three-leafed clover plant is the same, or the existence of the Fibonacci sequence[2] in a sunflower or conch shell.

Music Smart

Music and movement often work together, as demonstrated in the way Rachel's counting practice was enhanced as she recited in cadence with her stride. But music all on its own is powerful as well. Thus, whether you have an obviously music-smart child or are hoping to activate and enhance that smart in her, find a curriculum that uses music as a mathematical memory tool. On The Roadmap (homeschoolroadmap.org), many such products are labeled as "Delight-Directed/Guided Unschooling" on the Math charts and can also be found on the lists for Educational Media. Beyond these resources, you can make up little ditties of your own, such as the song I created—sung to the tune of "Twinkle, Twinkle Little Star"—to help my girls memorize our phone number and address.

Research has clearly demonstrated that listening to classical music and/or learning to play piano enhance people's mathematical reasoning skills. [3] So play classical music quietly in the background as your kids do their bookwork, or encourage a child to listen to classical music with her earbuds while doing math. Investigate the possibility of piano lessons, whether in your community or online via one of the providers listed on The Roadmap's chart for piano instruction, located within the site's Deluxe Charts Project.

Picture Smart

Picture-smart kids think with their eyes and with pictures. They are sensitive to visual details and have an ability to observe, transform, and re-create different aspects of the visual-spatial world. In the realm of math, you may be able to identify picture smart in a child who resonates far more with geometry-related content than with abstract (i.e., algebraic) concepts—it's easier for her to visualize the former than the latter—and in a child who responds well to the judicious use of a video-based math curriculum, such as *Teaching Textbooks*. As with body- and nature-smart children, picture-smart kids benefit from the use of manipulatives, but they might also gravitate toward "just" making representational drawings of math problems because they don't necessarily need to hold and touch their visual cues.

To help your picture-smart child learn to identify numbers and match the numerals to amounts, let her make flash cards showing a number on one side and pictures that she draws with the right amount on the other. Allow her to make similar flash cards for math facts and fractions, keeping in mind that it is the making of the tool—rather than drilling with premade cards—that really helps to cement the content into a child's mind. When working on word problems, encourage the child to sketch the scene being described, marking off relevant numbers somewhat to scale. And it's possible even with algebra to use self-made drawings to represent the equations before working the process to solve them. In fact, graphing tasks associated with advanced algebra and trigonometry generally make a great deal of sense to picture-smart kids even as they baffle others.

The key to all of this is remembering that the use of visuals is not cheating or somehow "less rigorous" than limiting a child to mental math. When we want a child to learn and retain something, we need (without bias) to meet the child where she's at.

People Smart

People-smart kids like to learn with other people. This might explain why your teen prefers sitting at the kitchen table to work on her geometry as you help her younger siblings with spelling and science. She's perfectly capable of doing the work on her own but actually becomes more productive when surrounded by family.

Similarly, a younger people-smart kid may seek regular confirmation from you that she's done her math correctly—even if she and you both know she has. There's certainly a balance between providing regular feedback and helping a child to grow in self-sufficiency, but people-smart kids really do need verbal affirmation and involvement from others in all their learning tasks, including math. A child's need for this kind of feedback will diminish as she matures, but parents must set the stage for independence by willingly offering their presence and feedback when the child is young.

Over the course of my homeschooling years, I saw the formation of all sorts of small co-ops—for everything from biology to Spanish to public speaking. Though I know of the existence of competitive homeschool math teams in larger cities, I've never heard of an actual learning co-op for math. Yet a math-oriented co-op—where a handful of kids all studying algebra or personal finance meets regularly to study together—would be a real blessing for people-smart kids.

Self Smart

In contrast, self-smart learners prefer to study alone and find group instruction stressful. For this reason, homeschooling as a whole is generally a positive experience for self-smart kids. It's not that homeschoolers are isolated—I long for the day when we can finally, once-and-for-all, disavow society of that myth! But we homeschoolers can be more intentional about social interaction. The fact that self-smart, home-educated kids can pick and choose when, where, how, and with whom to hang out enables them to relax and thrive.

Yet we do need to keep an eye on self-smart kids, perhaps in regard to math more than other subject areas. A self-smart child may prefer to figure things out on her own, and that's a good overall learning habit. However, because math knowledge builds upon itself, a kid who gets confused at some point but doesn't ask for help—as self-smart people sometimes tend to do—could end up struggling unnecessarily. Thus, the challenge for parents of a self-smart kid is to find a check-in method that respects the child's desire for space while still insuring she isn't getting lost in the content.

> *The challenge for parents of self-smart kids is to find a check-in method that respects the child's desire for space while still insuring she isn't getting lost in the content.*

Word Smart

Word smart seems at face value to be in direct opposition to math content—and, indeed, word-smart kids may struggle in math. But I recently asked Rachel—who is also highly word smart—what helped her with math or what aspects of math made most sense to her, and she immediately replied, "Word problems. I liked word problems." Well, that flies in the face of the commonly held view that everyone hates such problems! But word-smart people think with words, so it makes sense that they'd gravitate toward math couched in stories. In fact, a handful of curricular resources have been designed to help kids memorize math facts by presenting them

Create a personal smarts-for-my-kids reference guide.

in the context of stories and mnemonic devices. But—as with picture-oriented flash cards—a word-smart child can make this sort of practice tool for herself as well, either orally or in writing. For example, why not ask a child to tell a story to illustrate the fact that $4 + 4 = 8$ or that 5×2 (five sets of two) equals 10? Similarly, you can help a word-smart kid with more advanced math by talking through the various elements of a problem out loud, helping her to consciously verbalize what the various mathematical symbols mean and how they relate to each other in context.

A Personal Guide to Your Kid

By now you're getting familiar with the various smarts, and you're probably already homing in on the multiple intelligence strengths (and weaknesses) of your kids; I hope these few examples and ideas encourage you as you think about your kids' specific math-learning needs. Of course, my ideas aren't exhaustive—and you know your kids better than anyone else ever will—so I encourage you to grab a notebook (my guess is that you've got a large stash!) and make it your personal smarts-for-my-kids reference guide. Jot down the math ideas that have most resonated with you, and then add thoughts and ideas of your own. Keep it handy as you get ready to think about English language arts.

LANGUAGE ARTS:
The FOUNDATION Upon Which Much RELIES

Around the time I started working with my girls on counting, I decided it was time for Rachel to learn to read. And Abbie, just eleven-and-a-half months younger than Rachel, had repeatedly demonstrated a desire to "keep up." She'd walked at just eight months and decided to become potty-trained at one-and-a-half because her sister was learning. So I determined I might as well kill two proverbial birds with one stone and teach her too.

I quickly saw that Abbie was *cognitively* up to the task; she understood that letters "made sounds" and could readily remember which sounds went with what letters. The problem was, as I realized in hindsight, she wasn't *emotionally* ready. Thus, though she did what I asked with math and tackled penmanship like a champ, she pitched a fit every time I brought out the reading materials.

To say this bewildered me is a massive understatement. Abbie was generally the more obedient of the two girls, and she'd clearly been demonstrating an ability to manage phonics. It made no sense to me that she cried and yelled at the sight of the reading booklets.

I wondered if I should set it aside for a time. But I didn't want to send her the message that having a tantrum would get her what she wanted. So I kept trying but also began praying for guidance.

A few weeks later—after Abbie had been continuing to understand the concepts but also continuing to whine and fuss—I pulled out the material and called her to the table. I'll never forget how she decisively crossed her arms, stomped her little foot, and scolded me.

We educate our kids according to each one's demonstrated readiness rather than following arbitrary cultural norms.

"Momma! I just wanna be four!"

I knew in my gut that God had delivered an answer to my prayers through Abbie herself. She was right. No four-year-old "has to" read. It didn't matter that Abbie was cognitively able. Her behavior—so otherwise out-of-character for her—indicated that she simply wasn't ready, no matter how much I thought she was.

We kept doing math and penmanship. But I boxed up the phonics stuff and told her we'd try again after her next birthday unless she said she was ready sooner.

And one day eight months later—a month before her birthday—she came to me and matter-of-factly announced, "I'm ready now, Momma."

I winced; I didn't relish the thought of more tantrums. But I pulled out the kit—the same material as before—and sat down with her to try. And guess what? Abbie was right! She *was* ready! She breezed through the lessons, this time with peace and joy instead of angst and tears. She took to reading so well that by the time she was seven she was devouring books written with eleven-year-olds in mind.

This story demonstrates an incredibly important principle: it's imperative that we educate our kids according to each one's *demonstrated readiness* rather than following arbitrary cultural norms—or what the schools do. There is *nothing* hard-wired into the human brain requiring that all children learn to read at five (or four)! Some are ready at about that age, and others can learn earlier. But many are not ready until later, sometimes much later.

Some children have legitimate learning disabilities that hinder their ability to read well. But the reason schools force the issue at around five—trying to make all kids learn to read at the same time—has nothing to do with science. It's only to simplify the task of managing large groups of children at one time. At home we avoid that pressure; we have the privilege of watching and waiting. A child who is ready to learn to read will show interest in following along with the words in read-aloud books, will regularly ask what words around him say, and will pick up on phonics instruction with relative ease and without undue stress. We save ourselves and our kids a lot of grief if we wait until we see each child's actual readiness.

We can also utilize kids' inherent smarts to help with the task of learning to read—as well as with the other things floating in the big bucket of skills we call "language arts."

Language arts as an entity is comprised of all the skills that enable us to listen, speak, read, and write well. Broken into recognizable subtopics, it includes learning to read (i.e., phonics), penmanship, spelling, grammar, reading to learn (comprehension) and literary analysis, written composition, public speaking, and vocabulary. Obviously, that's a huge body of knowledge! And, though we certainly don't need to cover it all at one time,[1] it's a vastly important one. In fact, being able to comprehend others' communication and communicate clearly ourselves underpins virtually every other content area and ultimately contributes to a healthy, productive adult life.

Word Smart

Remember how logic-smart kids often take to math naturally? The same can be said, broadly speaking, for word-smart children and language arts. If you have a child who loves reading (or being read to), writing, and speaking, and who listens intently, he is very likely word smart. As a result, many—although maybe not all—language arts–related skills come to him with relative ease. Depending on his overall smarts profile, a word-smart child will still require direct instruction in language arts, but he'll probably be able to master some areas instinctively—i.e., a "natural speller" is most certainly word-smart—and will enjoy working with words in one way or another.

Logic Smart

Rachel is word smart, but she was a rather late bloomer with reading, and spelling drove her bonkers. We eventually found *Pathway Reading* (Milestone Books) and *All About Spelling* (All About Learning Press), which worked well for both girls, yet spelling didn't click for Rachel until she was about thirteen. Even Kathy Koch, who's written six books to date, considers herself a struggling speller!

The probable root cause of spelling difficulty? Logic smart. As Pocahontas exclaimed in an animated movie my girls used to watch, "English needs to be fixed!"[2]

Pocahontas is right. In contrast to some other languages (for example, Spanish), English is very *illogical*. English is a mishmash of several other languages, so its "rules"—for decoding words, spelling, and even grammatical constructs—are broken as often as they're kept.[3] Naturally, this frustrates logic-smart kids. Unfortunately, there's little we can do about it because, though languages change over time, it's unlikely that linguists will choose overnight to eliminate the letter *c* from the alphabet (why do we need it when *k* and *s* can do the job?) to appease discouraged logic-smart learners.

But I've found that acknowledging the craziness of the English language—rather than blaming a child for not knowing how to sound out a word, having "bad spelling," or using the wrong preposition—helps a lot. When a child knows his error stems from assuming some logic where English falls short, he'll be more motivated to persevere. Utilizing a method for phonics and spelling instruction that breaks things down as logically as possible (for example, the Orton-Gillingham approach)[4] can also go a long way toward helping a logic-smart kid cope with our language.

I'm a big fan of copywork and transcription[5] as tools for practicing penmanship—and as an indirect way of improving vocabulary and modeling correct grammar and spelling. In terms of the smarts, copywork is easily customizable to suit any particular child's strengths. For example, a logic-smart kid can copy game instructions, favorite recipes, and other non-fiction texts. Or you can hand him a set of words—maybe his spelling list—and instruct him to chart them into logical categories as he copies.

In regard to literacy, once a child knows how to read, I recommend a method I call Readers' Workshop rather than using premade literature curricula.[6] This approach allows kids to choose—within broad parameters set by a parent—which material to read and how to demonstrate comprehension of its content. It meshes beautifully with multiple intelligences by granting kids agency. Logic-smart kids, for instance, tend to pick non-fiction texts over novels, and you can embrace their natural inclination, and respect their natural "wiring," using the Workshop philosophy.

Diagramming was the bane of my existence in school—and it's not the only way to learn grammar[7]—but logic-smart kids embrace it because diagramming is all about categorizing parts of speech. Similarly, these kids enjoy vocabulary activities—such as Norman Lewis's book *Word Power Made Easy* or *Word Up!* (Compass Classroom)—which focus on learning the meanings of various roots and affixes.

In terms of written composition, a logic-smart child may gravitate to some kinds of writing more than others. It's good to remember that creative writing—composing fictional stories and poems—is not a life skill. Some children and teens—word-smart kids and others—love creative writing. Logic-smart kids probably won't. And, because one doesn't *need* to write poetry or fiction to lead a productive, happy life, there's no need to badger a logic-smart child into it. Instead, focus with them (and other kids) on the process of *expository* writing—that is, non-fiction written to explain, describe, inform, or persuade.[8] And to encourage the development of public presentation skills, find or create a debate club in which your logic-smart child can participate.

Picture Smart

Kids of all ages and every smarts profile benefit from being read to long after they've learned to decode and comprehend for themselves.[9] But the practice can be particularly powerful for picture-smart kids, who think with images and can readily visualize. As you allow a picture-smart child to see the text, he may pick up on learning to read rather easily. In fact, though I'm a proponent of providing phonics instruction, picture-smart kids are more apt to be whole-to-part thinkers, able to see and remember whole words as "pictures" in their brains. Thus, they benefit from reading in context (learning to read via actual stories) rather than focusing solely on "sounding out" isolated words.

Picture-smart kids usually like to draw and color, which develops their fine-motor skills and often enables them to master penmanship quickly and happily. For example, Abbie colored well at a very young age and referred to cursive as "princess writing" because she loved it so much. Allow picture-smart children to choose copywork texts from favorite picture books so they can enjoy the artwork as they write.

For both handwriting and spelling practice, picture-smart kids may enjoy using pens with different ink colors. To help them master both phonics and spelling, encourage them to build words on the fridge with colored magnets, to design their own illustrated flash cards, and to use Kathy's "close your eyes and see" method.[10] Similarly, support kids' picture smart while learning vocabulary by letting them create illustrated personal dictionaries.

Picture-smart learners often resonate with diagramming to learn grammar, but for a different reason from their logic-smart siblings. For these kids, the diagrams stick in their brains as pictures, enabling them to visualize the content.

With Readers' Workshop, picture-smart kids gravitate toward novels bursting with expressive language and detailed descriptions; in fact, they may be most apt—along with word-smart kids—to voluntarily choose old classics. In responding to what they've read, allow these kids to create artwork—illustrated picture-book versions of novels, posters, etc.—instead of book reports. They can practice public speaking skills by describing their projects during evening family time.

Picture-smart kids may excel at expository writing because of their ability to visualize and describe, but they'll probably prefer mind mapping[11] over traditional outlining in their planning phase. Along with word-smart kids, those with a high level of picture smart may also enjoy creative writing. Encourage their endeavors and offer helpful aids—such as *Spilling Ink: A Young Writer's Handbook* (Square Fish)—if asked. But you might very well find that too much "curriculum" can squelch the success of those wired to write poems, stories, and novels. In reality, they don't always need much formal instruction.

Nature Smart

Nature-smart learners share traits with both logic- and picture-smart kids. They look for patterns, similar in some ways to their logic-smart peers, and they enjoy observing the way picture-smart kids do. They're apt, like those with logic smart, to be frustrated by the inconsistencies in the English language, so many of the same techniques will help them. But their powers of observation may soften that blow since they may see patterns in words on the page—in phonics, spelling, and vocabulary.

When working on penmanship, allow nature-smart kids to choose copywork texts from nature-oriented books you find at the library or via a series such as the Christian Liberty Press Nature Readers. Encourage them to seek out nature-themed books—both fiction and non-fiction—for Readers' Workshop. Likewise, let them write about nature-oriented themes rather than topics you assign; I don't know how she endured it, but one of my English teachers graciously allowed me to write about nothing but cats for an entire year! With the writing

As homeschoolers, we have freedom to allow our kids to study in a variety of environments.

process, exact topics can be flexible as you hang onto the goal of teaching children to write for different purposes and master the steps in the writing process itself.

One of the most effective techniques for helping nature-smart kids with all learning tasks is allowing them to be outside—or at least near windows that enable them to see outside—as much as possible. Being outdoors in the yard or down by the creek might distract some kids, so you may want to use the gift of time outdoors judiciously, as a motivational tool. But with guidance and practice, your nature-smart child may focus on reading, spelling, and writing more intently when perched in a favorite tree or sprawled on the lawn. As homeschoolers, we have freedom to allow our kids to study in a variety of environments; we should take advantage of that perk.

Music Smart

Music-smart kids think with rhythm and melodies. Thus, they may enjoy working on their language arts lessons while listening to background music, especially classical or other reflective instrumental styles (without vocal lyrics). Of course, if the music distracts, it can be used as a reward rather than a default study mode. Experiment to see what works for your child or teen.

These kids may benefit when learning to read and spell by clapping out syllables or using volume cues (for example, whispering the name of a silent letter when spelling aloud). Similarly, they can create chants of their own (similar to the cadence we use when spelling the word "Mississippi") or make up songs to remember vocabulary words.

For copywork, help music-smart learners find uplifting song lyrics, such as the words of hymns, or let them choose from among biblical psalms. As a bonus, this will naturally provide solid theological content, almost by osmosis.

Music-smart kids may enjoy reading biographies about composers and musicians. In response to their reading, encourage them to try composing their own related songs. They may gravitate toward writing poetry—song lyrics without music—so they might need extra encouragement and instruction when tackling prose (essays, reports, and research papers). But, again, if we allow kids to write about topics of personal interest—such as "Beethoven's Childhood" or "Louisiana in the Jazz Age"—we increase their motivation to dig in and learn the process.

Voice lessons would also be an excellent investment. A good voice teacher instructs in diction and projection as well as how to use the diaphragm and vocal cords. A child or teen who can sing in front of a crowd will gain the confidence to speak in public as well.

Body Smart

Body-smart kids think when they move. If that has included an interest in coloring or other fine-motor activities (such as building with Legos), a body-smart child may pick up on penmanship at an early age. However, if he has more affinity for large-motor activities, he may struggle with sitting down to write. If you feel he's developmentally ready, two strategies may help. First, use something other than pen and paper—for example, show him how to form letters with his finger in sand or cocoa powder spread on a baking sheet. Second, start with cursive rather than manuscript-style—A Beka and Cursive First are two providers that introduce penmanship via cursive—because the "flow" of cursive puts less strain on finger muscles while concurrently engaging more arm muscles. But it may be better to simply wait until the child shows readiness (more fine-motor control and more patience with sitting for short stints). As homeschoolers, we get to mold our lessons to the needs of the child, not the other way around.

The same can be said with learning to read. But because body-smart kids respond to touch, another technique to consider is buddy-reading.[12] Your body-smart child who is developmentally ready to read will respond more positively to cuddling on the couch with you than to sitting across from you at the dining room table.

In terms of spelling and grammar, use resources—such as *All About Spelling* (All About Learning Press), *Winston Grammar* (Precious Memories), or Dianne Craft's materials—that incorporate even simple actions like moving letter tiles and word cards or looking up while thinking about how to spell tricky words. Another option would be to use colored magnets and homemade parts-of-speech cards on your refrigerator or a magnetic white board.

For Readers' Workshop, allow your body-smart kid to read in "odd" locations or positions; as a girl, my mother-in-law read upside down on the couch, her feet draped over the back of the sofa and her head hanging over the edge! And encourage body-smart kids to create projects—dioramas, models of key objects, puppets, costumes that main characters would have worn—in response to what they read. Building and designing are legitimate ways to evaluate a child's comprehension of books.

Don't worry if your body-smart teen moves when composing an essay or short story. In fact, consider investing in voice-to-text software he can use at the computer while bouncing on his exercise ball or while meandering around the house or yard, phone in hand. Body-smart people think while they're moving; your body-smart kid will write more coherently if you let him move as he composes.

Finally, consider involving your body-smart kid in theater productions, either through a homeschool group or community program. Being involved in drama is an excellent way to engage such kids in the language arts, particularly public speaking.

People Smart

People-smart kids will also relish the buddy-reading technique, as well as other opportunities to learn while getting feedback from others. For example, when one of my girls needed regular visits to a chiropractor, I instituted the practice of buddy-spelling, having the girls drill spelling words with each other during our drives to and from.

Helping homeschooled kids become independent, self-directed learners is valuable. But people-smart learners need more parental interaction than some other kids, and it's important to accept that reality. Though we can encourage independence where appropriate—such as a child being able to practice penmanship on his own after he knows how to form the letters—we want to work with and not against our kids' hard-wired smarts. For example, a people-smart kid will thrive with spelling, grammar, and vocabulary curricula that require one-on-one direct instruction but may flounder if given a workbook and told, "Go do your grammar."

In responding to literature, people-smart kids delight in making oral presentations to their families and writing and performing skits related to what they've read. You might also find or launch a book club in which your people-smart child and similar-aged peers read and discuss books together. And, as with logic- and body-smart kids, people-smart learners thrive in debate clubs and drama programs.

Self Smart

In contrast, self-smart kids may struggle if you sign them up for that kind of group activity. Sometimes—because being able to interact with others is an important life skill—it is wise to nudge our self-smart children into practicing being part of a group. But we must do that carefully. Pray for discernment to know the difference between pushing too hard or nudging judiciously.

In terms of other literacy skills, self-smart kids may enjoy listening to audio books before they learn to read. You can encourage their ability to decode by directing them to follow along with written texts as they listen. These are also the kids who—when sufficiently literate—prefer to work on vocabulary, grammar, and spelling by themselves.

Because self-smart learners enjoy inward reflection, they'll like using Bible verses and poetry for copywork. Also consider allowing a self-smart child to create personal spelling lists rather than assigning words to him. Likewise, self-smart kids love the personal choice afforded to them via the Readers' Workshop approach and appreciate being allowed to choose their own topics for written composition, whether expository or creative. You might even tackle workshop responses and writing at the same time by encouraging a self-smart kid to create a book review blog. While private and personal on the one hand, blogging gets self-smart kids out "into the world" in a way that feels less intimidating than speech, debate, and drama clubs.

Again, it's all about working with—not against—the way a child has been wired.

Language Arts and Your Specific Children

Whew! That's a lot of information to soak in. So before you move on, pull out the smarts reference guide you've started and create a page for language arts. Scan through this chapter for noteworthy ideas and add your own thoughts as well. And, since language forms the foundation for so much other content, be prepared to cycle back here to review these ideas in relation to other subject areas as we proceed.

SCIENCE:
INVESTIGATE
Your Options

"Mom, will water evaporate faster from a cup that has a cover on it or from one that doesn't?"

This is just one of many questions with which my friend Kelly's younger son has peppered his parents since he was very young. Kelly and her husband, Curt, originally did their best to immediately answer Jacob's questions based on their own knowledge. However, they quickly realized that many of his questions required that they do a bit of research and learn alongside him.

The questions Jacob asked tended to relate to matters of science, math, and faith. As he approached kindergarten age, Kelly discerned that the questions pointed to Jacob's logic smart. She also realized that she had a tremendous opportunity to harness his questions to nurture his desire to learn and also guide his education in particular subjects.

The family's science learning over the past few years has been primarily guided by the questions Jacob asks about the world around him. Now, though, instead of just providing answers, Curt and Kelly respond with, "Let's do an experiment and find out," or "Let's read a book about it and learn together." The way God has designed Jacob to be logic smart has led to learning adventures the family may never have otherwise pursued.

Homeschoolers—either when first starting out or when entering a new leg of the journey (such as beginning the high school years)—regularly ask each other for input about scheduling: "What's the best daily schedule? Do you use block scheduling? Do you loop? Do we have to follow the local school's schedule? Should we school year-round?"[1]

Flexing when necessary must be an easily accessible tool in a Mother's Toolkit.

My answer is to challenge a parent to consider what might work best for her particular family. Simply put, there is no "best" schedule—daily, weekly, or annually. Just as with curriculum, what works for one family may be a complete bust for another. Thus, the best way to set a routine for your family is to analyze the real needs of each family member, figure out an initial game plan, try out a possible schedule, and then (most importantly) tweak and adjust as needed. In all that, the one set point to which I believe all homeschoolers should adhere is flexibility.

My husband will laugh when he reads that because his nickname for me is "Rou-Tina." The moniker carries truth—I do like consistency—but I've learned that flexing when necessary must be an easily accessible tool in my Mother's Toolkit—and all the more so as a homeschooler.

Science might encourage tangents because, by its very nature, science is all about asking questions.

This is important simply because "life" happens. Like it or not, the baby *will* blow out her diaper just as you're heading out the door to homeschool art class. The flu *will* wend its way through your entire family the week before a vacation, putting you doubly behind. Your teen *will* sustain a concussion at soccer practice right before the PSAT test day.

Flexibility also makes room for the beautiful rabbit trails that truly bless the homeschool life—like when Jacob inquired about evaporating water, or when your child wonders why the night sky looks like a bowl or asks if Jesus had straight or curly hair. Planning of some sort—however that might look for you—helps direct us as we guide our kids' educational journeys. But leaving margin— each day, week, and year—for the unexpected learning detours is a homeschool hallmark we should embrace.

Of all the subject areas, science might encourage the majority of tangents—perhaps because science, by its very nature, is all about asking questions. And the question on your mind today may be: How can I apply my kids' smarts strengths to science?

Nature Smart

As with logic smart and math, or word smart and language arts, nature-smart kids often excel in scientific fields that focus on the natural world—biology (botany, human anatomy and physiology, zoology), meteorology, and environmental science. Nature-smart kids love exploring outside—formally or informally—even in urban settings and benefit from raising pets and keeping gardens. If you are homesteading (gardening and/or raising your own animals, etc., to be more self-sufficient and environmentally conscientious) along with homeschooling, your kids are likely steeped in opportunities to grow their nature smart.

As mentioned previously, you can harness nature smart as a motivational tool by allowing kids wired in this vein to read and write about relevant topics of interest. And, even if you don't ascribe entirely to her approaches, utilizing Charlotte Mason's nature study technique will go a long way toward maximizing nature smart in all your kids.[2]

That said, don't expect your nature-smart child to love every type of science. In fact, chemistry, physics, and other applied science (STEM)[3] may not appeal to your nature-smart kid unless she also has a high degree of logic smart. And that's okay. While we should help our kids develop a layman's understanding of many subject areas—and might use a child's strengths to get at topics she is less motivated to learn—no one can or should be an expert in everything. My girls—one of whom is quite nature-smart but neither of whom has much interest in science—are good examples of this. For their high school studies, we covered basic chemistry and physics, not the more-detailed coursework I'd have used if they were interested in science-oriented careers. That wasn't a cop-out on my part; it was conscious customization.

Logic Smart

Logic-smart kids are also apt to be drawn to science of all sorts because of how they're wired to ask questions. The basis of scientific inquiry, the scientific method, is grounded in the practice of asking a question (making a hypothesis) and then working (experimenting) to find evidence-based answers.

Their inquiring minds may make logic-smart kids more frustrated by typical (school-style) science curricula, which require them to passively read about various topics, spit back cookie-cutter answers on conventional tests, and occasionally follow carefully prescribed steps to complete basic experiments. Project-based learning—an active, hands-on approach giving learners the opportunity to use inductive as well as deductive reasoning and experiment frequently—and resources using the Classical approach, particularly during the Logic and Rhetoric stages, are better fits for these kids. Both styles are included in The Roadmap's Deluxe Charts Project, enabling you to see at a glance which curricula might suit your logic-smart child.

Self Smart

According to Kathy Koch, "Self-smart children want to understand things in depth."[4] Therefore, the types of science resources that resonate with logic-smart kids—that is, those encouraging inductive as well as deductive reasoning—will appeal to these kids too. A self-smart child may prefer to work through learning tasks on her own, and she'll want to take her time, ensuring that she deeply understands various concepts.

Consider having a self-smart child keep a science journal—in a notebook or on a blog—to reflect on each day's science activities. She can summarize concepts she encounters when reading a section in a science book or watching a video lesson. She can evaluate the outcome of an experiment she performs. She can connect a scientific theory with her own observations of the world around her. Ask her to share her entries with you on a regular basis—not necessarily daily but often enough for you to see her progression of thought—and take time to discuss them, one-on-one. If you've never before tried such journaling, you'll likely be amazed at the depth of thought your self-smart child expresses simply because you've given her space and time to do so.

People Smart

People-smart kids thrive in science-based co-ops or kitchen-table dissection groups, where they can work together with others— homeschooled peers, siblings, or a parent—and then discuss their findings and conclusions. However, a people-smart kid may balk at writing up lab reports or taking school-style tests ("But, Mom, we discussed this together for an hour. Why do I have to write it up too?"). And, honestly, she may have a point!

Though "lab reports" have a place as an occasionally valuable scientific exercise, and though conventional tests might feel comfortable to some kids, neither is necessarily the only or best way to evaluate a child's learning. Schools emphasize those tools for convenience-sake within that setting. For example, a chemistry teacher who sees 150 kids a day can't possibly have personalized discussions with each student, yet he needs some way to demonstrate whether or not the kids have grasped various concepts. But in real life outside of school—in the workforce and in family life—collaborative discussion reigns. Written reports are sometimes required but not always. And no one in a science lab or office environment takes bubble-tests or essay exams. With that in mind, you can legitimately evaluate your child's understanding of scientific concepts simply by talking with her; in fact, doing so with a people-smart child will enhance her learning and garner a more thorough evaluation than making her write ten lab reports.

Word Smart

In contrast to logic-smart kids, those with a high level of word smart are often quite satisfied to learn science from reading alone, whether via conventional textbooks or Charlotte Mason–oriented living books.[5] They probably won't mind taking multiple-choice tests, responding to essay questions, or even writing lab reports. What may annoy them is doing experiments.

You have the freedom and authority to customize for your kids, too, even when doing so goes against conventional norms.

I discovered during my high school years that I love doing dissections. Studying the specimens' body systems fascinated me and, in fact, increased my love of animals. When I became a mom and we began homeschooling, I enjoyed hearing about the dissection activities of my friends with older kids and looked forward to experiencing that with the girls.

Fast forward to their middle and high school years, though, and it had become apparent that neither of the girls was called toward the sciences. Rachel may have found dissection mildly interesting, but Abbie—who eventually became a vegetarian—was appalled at the idea. Because they are word smart on the one hand and ambivalent about science on the other, both were completely content to learn what I required of them by reading, journaling, and engaging in discussion. I could have stretched them by attempting dissection, and I did consider requiring it. In the end, though, I made the call—as the one who knows my kids better than anyone else and as the legal administrator of our home-based educational program—to skip it. You have the freedom and authority to customize for your kids, too, even when doing so goes against conventional norms.

Picture Smart

A picture-smart kid can thrive in the sciences if you allow her to learn through texts with vibrant images and diagrams as well as excellent web-based and video content. For example, among the myriad possibilities listed on The Roadmap, I've heard from many homeschoolers whose kids (of all ages) still love and learn from the old *Moody Science Classics* videos. It's also helpful to allow a picture-smart learner to demonstrate her understanding through drawings and diagrams.

I'm actually very word smart, but I'm picture smart too. I rewrote my high school science notes every night, turning my initial hasty scrawls into neatly written lists and charts and adding my own full-color sketches as I went. I wanted my notes to look beautiful, and I quickly realized that the act of recopying was a study skill. I also loved doing lab drawings. I willingly spent hours on them, mastering anatomical terminology and mentally reviewing related physiology as I carefully labeled and colored each sketch. I was learning in a public school, so I also had to take the requisite exams, but I found I didn't need to cram before the tests. The facts and concepts had been embedded into my brain as I carefully prepared diagrams.

Music Smart

Though a classical music fan, I don't remember listening to it while I did my science drawings—but I could have, as a means of putting my music smart to use as another study aid. Unfortunately, the one resource I know of that has developed jingles to help kids remember scientific ideas has chosen to align its content with the Common Core and Next Generation Science Standards, initiatives I'd personally rather not endorse.[6]

However, your music-smart child can create personalized study-tool ditties and rhymes using simple and familiar melodies or new tunes she composes herself. You can even choose to think way outside the school-style box by using her songs—rather than tests or reports—to evaluate her comprehension of the content.

Body Smart

Any activity that incorporates movement or touch can help a body-smart child with science: nature walks (especially if they involve collecting specimens), setting up and performing lab experiments, doing dissections, listening to audiobook versions of science texts while mowing the lawn or taking a walk around the block, using the "skywriting" technique described by Kathy Koch when reviewing scientific terminology,[7] even playing science-oriented board and card games. It all "counts" as real, legitimate ways to encourage a body-smart kid or teen to learn any science-based concept.

Inquire and Experiment

Science is built on the foundation of inquiry and experimentation—that is, curiosity that causes a person to ask questions about the world around her and investigation to try to answer those questions. As a homeschool parent, you have, in a way, taken on the role of social scientist, intent on discovering the ways each of your children learns best. Each chapter in this book should further refine the image of your kids' smarts profiles in your own mind while sparking your interest in customizing each one's education based on that profile. So make some notes (pictures optional!) in your handy-dandy smarts reference guide—your smarts lab manual, if you will—in relation to the science you want your kids to know and use.

SOCIAL STUDIES:
Who in
the WORLD

Helen, a member of a small Wisconsin-based homeschool group I moderate,[1] uses a variety of tabletop games as a major component of her family's homeschool curriculum. Helen, her husband, and their kids have always loved unique board games, but they plunged into the world of game-schooling because of their daughter Beth.

Beth was born with unique challenges and has been diagnosed with autism spectrum disorder. She's extremely bright, always playing and pretending, and dives deeply into her imaginary worlds. But at a certain point, Helen began wrestling with how to pull Beth out of those worlds long enough to help her learn to read, write, and count. Beth was getting older, beyond the age when children typically learn to read, and Helen was scared and frustrated. She didn't want to squash Beth's love of learning or inhibit her amazing imagination but needed a way to engage Beth in academic learning.

Then one day it clicked. When Helen and Beth played games together—including some social studies-oriented favorites such as *Catan* and *Ticket to Ride*—Helen noticed that Beth almost always won. In particular, Helen noted that it was nearly impossible for Beth to lose when they played games based on the use of visual patterning or logic. Beth mapped out game plans in her head, memorized every card despite being unable to read them, and came up with complex strategies.

There's far more to "curriculum" than textbooks.

This revelation led Helen's husband on a hunt for the best games around.[2] Within weeks of launching into a daily regimen of concentrated game-play, Beth went from barely putting sounds together to continuously learning to read new words. Beth's reading tutor noticed Beth's markedly increased motivation to try harder and longer words, too. Helen also saw Beth's math skills skyrocket; Beth quickly jumped from struggling to count to twenty, to skip counting and adding large numbers in her head. In fact, Beth even began correcting Helen's addition!

When Helen and her husband recognized and locked in on Beth's logic-, picture-, and nature-smart strengths, Beth gained confidence to stretch in areas where she had felt weak. As a side benefit, Helen has been strengthening her own smarts as she plays new games with Beth and her other children.

Helen's story illustrates a little homeschool secret of which many are unaware: there's far more to "curriculum" than textbooks! According to Dictionary.com, *curriculum* is simply "the aggregate of courses of study given in a school" and is synonymous with "educational program" and "program of study." The term *curriculum* is *not* a synonym for *textbook*. Instead, it actually suggests the use of *any* resources that advance a child's academic development, not just conventional, school-style material. As if to illustrate this reality, the owner of Eclectic Homeschooling has created a Homeschool Philosophies Quiz identifying no fewer than ten distinct homeschool learning approaches, each of which suggests the use of a unique mix of resources and activities to accomplish its goals. [3]

Don't get me wrong. Despite what some kids think, textbooks aren't evil. The majority of providers I list and chart on The Roadmap employ what I call a "Traditional/School-Style" approach using conventional material in either a print-based format or online, and that works—in one shape or form—for some kids. But many children and teens actually thrive using various nontraditional resources. And even those who tolerate or enjoy textbooks can benefit from some diversity in their learning

We have the freedom at home to expand our horizons beyond the conventional.

endeavors. We have the freedom at home to expand our horizons beyond the conventional. Actually, planning in terms of kids' multiple intelligence strengths *requires* us to get out of the school-style box in which we tend to live.

The term *social studies* as a subject-area label carries multiple possible connotations. But most contemporary homeschoolers simply think of the phrase as a generalization referring to several subtopics—especially history, geography, civics, and economics.[4] Thus, I'll use that common understanding of the phrase going forward.

People Smart

The focus of math is numbers. The language arts emphasize words, and science mainly homes in on non-human components of the physical world. In contrast, the social studies zoom in on *people* in one way or another—their history, their physical and cultural environments, their forms of government, and their means of sustaining themselves on the planet. For that reason, it's not far-fetched to suggest that people smart is particularly relevant to this subject area.

People-smart learners are, after all, able to discern and then respond to the moods, intentions, and desires of others, and they can get inside other people's heads and view the world from other perspectives. Thus—whether we're thinking about how others in the world right now live, or about how people lived in the past—people-smart kids are apt to be drawn to social studies-related topics. The key to sustaining their natural interest may rest in applying their other smarts strengths to learning activities.

Word Smart

You might think word-smart kids would be the easiest to motivate simply because the majority of social studies curricula is text-based; word-smart kids like to read, so reading about civics, economics, history, and geography should be a no-brainer. But word-smart kids won't read just anything. They'll tune out of boring, poorly written books even more quickly than the next kid.

The good news for homeschoolers is that helping kids gain a grasp on civics and accurate history in particular has been a hallmark of the modern homeschool movement. And many homeschool publishers have intentionally worked to think beyond school-style social studies textbooks in order to create material that's actually interesting. For example, several publishers (BiblioPlan, Master Books, The Mystery of History, Nothing New Press, Tapestry of Grace, and TruthQuest History) have incorporated primary sources, engaging prose, and living books into their history curricula. And one publisher—Diana Waring—has even built her world history material directly around the eight smarts! The even better news is that literature publishers love history and geography! Thus, hundreds upon hundreds of picture and chapter books have been written for kids of all ages about various historical figures and events, and also about the physical and cultural geography of virtually every inch (above and below sea level!) of the earth. Homeschool parents need to vet for accuracy any literature that includes the stories of real people from the past, but historical fiction can be put to good use in the social studies because its authors take great pains to paint historically and geographically accurate pictures with their words.

Picture Smart

Homeschool social studies curricula is not limited to books; there are many well-done video resources with which to engage your picture-smart kids. When my girls were young, they loved NEST Animated DVDs, American Girl movies, and Liberty's Kids. During their high school years, we used History2U, an engaging DVD series, as the basis for their American history credit, and addressed economics via a video program called *Economics for Everybody*. PragerU and Hillsdale College offer free video-based civics lessons.

And Hollywood loves history! Hundreds of movies have been produced about various historical events over the years, many of them appropriate for kids and teens. Sometimes movie producers take liberty with historical facts—but we can still watch and discuss with our kids some of the documentaries and fictionalized movies set in the past and in other countries. In fact, doing so gives us opportunity to help them develop independent research skills and an ability to distinguish between fact and fiction.

We can also use picture smart to evaluate our kids' understanding of social-studies topics. For example, my daughters made history-based scrapbooks—theirs are physical books, but we could have created blogs instead—to demonstrate their comprehension of both American and world history. Each spread of each book includes a summary of the topic written by one of the girls, as well as relevant images she had to research. Each scrapbook is a testament to all that the girls studied and will far outlive any paper-and-pencil test I may have given instead.

Body Smart

The girls and I enjoyed The Mystery of History, a world history curriculum, so much that they went through all four of its volumes twice. They chose it over other options during their high school years and used it as the impetus for creating their world history scrapbooks. The first time through, though, happened when they were younger and I still directly facilitated their studies. I liked many things about the series, especially its regular inclusion of hands-on learning projects, of which I scheduled at least one every week. My favorite was creating replicas of the purple cloth Lydia from the New Testament may have woven, complete with a smell similar to what would have emanated from the dye Lydia gleaned from Mediterranean snails!

In fact, creating projects is critical to maximizing the learning endeavors of body-smart learners. Whether you use pre-packaged curricula, search out ideas on Pinterest, or work with your body-smart child to come up with his own projects, you'll want to do more than assign textbook pages, review questions, and standardized tests if you want him to fully engage with social-studies topics.

Music Smart

Music-smart kids like to make, listen to, and learn about music. You can easily use this strength to help them learn history and geography by centering your studies around music. For example, choose a representative composer from a particular era of history and study his biography and then his music. Listen intentionally to several pieces written by him, learn about the style into which it falls—is it baroque, classical, romantic?—and keep the music on in the background while going about your day. If possible, attend a live concert in which the composer's work will be performed. Consider having your child learn to play one of the pieces on his instrument of choice. Then use the composer as the starting point—like a rock thrown into a pond sending out ripples—to learn more about other history related to the era in which the composer lived. You can also do this with geography, beginning by investigating music associated with a particular people group and spreading out from there.

Another starting point for music-oriented unit study is musical theater—both live performances and video versions. As with historical fiction and history- or geography-themed movies, take care to help your kids distinguish between fact and fiction. But for a music-smart kid, watching *South Pacific* can be a legitimate rock-in-the-pond by which to begin a study of World War II, and seeing a production of *Les Misérables* at a local theater will pique his interest in the era surrounding the French Revolution or French culture in general.

Self Smart

Self-smart kids are reflective and tend to search for connections between their learning endeavors and their own lives. More than other kids, highly self-smart children and teens tune out if they feel a topic "isn't relevant." To a certain extent, we must help such kids get out of their own heads and grow in character—to realize the world doesn't revolve around them—so it's okay if they don't always feel they can "relate" to something you've asked them to study. However, self smart can be a powerful tool to employ in the social studies.

Encourage your self-smart child to consider—and talk, draw, or write about—ways in which he is the same as and different from various historical figures. Guide him to reflect about how cultural practices—the food people eat, the clothing they wear, their dwelling places—are similar to or different from his own. Pique his interest in civics by helping him become involved in governance at the local level—for example, lobbying the city council to build a new skate park or spending part of a day shadowing the mayor—and make economics personal by helping him start his own small business (even as a pre-teen!). Later, as he learns about the political and macroeconomic systems in your state and country, ask him to compare and contrast them to current norms in other countries as well as historical practices in past eras.

Logic Smart

Remember Beth and her games? Board, card, and even digital games engage logic-smart kids because they require asking and answering questions and the development of critical thinking strategies. When we use games that revolve around social studies topics—Civitas, The Classical Historian, The Constitution Quest Game, Passport to Culture, Professor Noggin, and We the People Fight Tyranny are a few that come to mind—logic-smart kids are able to more easily embed that knowledge in their brains.

Another way to engage kids' logic smart is through research projects. Logic-smart kids chafe at being spoon-fed; they want to find answers to their own questions rather than reading someone else's summaries. Run with that strength by letting logic-smart kids list questions about any social studies-related topic and then dig in—to a variety of resources, including primary source material—to find answers. The beauty of this approach with a logic-smart kid is that his questions won't end. One bit of research will bring more questions to mind. Before you know it, your "King of Rabbit Trails" will have a broad and deep understanding in social studies.

Nature Smart

The value of games in Beth's learning came from the activation of her picture-, logic- *and* nature-smart. At first glance, this may seem odd—tabletop games are usually played indoors, and social studies-themed games won't often (with the exception, perhaps, of games about physical geography) include any reference to flora and fauna. But remember that nature smart also includes the ability to see and create patterns, both of which are important game-play skills.

Another way to engage a nature-smart child in social studies is to take trips, big and small. My family undertook two major excursions as the girls were growing up—a Laura Ingalls Tour in 2008 and an Early American History Tour in 2014. Jeff also led them and a team of teens from our local homeschool group on a mission trip to Trinidad in 2019.[5] The girls will always remember wading in *the* Plum Creek in Minnesota, donning colonial-style dresses my mother-in-law sewed for them to wear in Williamsburg, and touring the Temple in the Sea and doing homeless ministry in Trinidad. But even small outings—to the neighborhood fire station, a local botanical garden with an exhibit of native plants, or a zoo to see animals from around the world—make an impact.[6]

Activate Their Smarts

If you were to survey adults asking them to express their feelings about social studies, the vast majority would quickly answer, "Boring!" Too many had to endure the study of history, geography, civics, and economics in school only through dry textbooks and spit-back-the-right-answer exams. Their smarts were not activated—not even word smart, given the nature of much mainstream social studies material. But you have the opportunity as a homeschooler to engage all of your kids' smarts for the purpose of helping them to understand human history and current events. So pull out your notebook, and remind yourself of ways you're going to begin as early as today.

FINE ARTS:
Beautiful
ENDEAVORS

f you've read *8 Great Smarts*, you'll likely remember the powerful story Kathy Koch shares about Kristin, a gifted actress and dancer.[1] The story stood out to me because I knew Kristin; she and I were both students at the university where Kathy taught and involved in the campus InterVarsity Christian Fellowship chapter. I admired—even envied—Kristin's abilities, grace, and apparent confidence. I never dreamed that she doubted her own intelligence and wasn't healed of that misperception until she heard Kathy speak about the smarts almost ten years after her college graduation.

Though conventional schools offer art and music classes and often provide opportunities for kids to participate in extracurricular activities like plays, musicals, and forensics, those endeavors aren't ultimately valued in the system. In school culture, we applaud a good musical performance and compliment beautiful artwork displayed at the annual fine arts fair—and we know that participating in theater productions creates fond lifelong memories. But prevailing wisdom says that the truly "smart" kids excel in math, science, and language arts—the subjects that supposedly make them "career ready." Artistic talent is relegated to second-string importance (or maybe third, behind athletics); artistic kids are told to get their heads out of the clouds and focus on what "really matters."

Homeschoolers don't have to elevate logic and word smart above the others.

As Kathy points out, that's because the two smarts strengths emphasized, by design, in the traditional school system are word and logic.[2] Kids who have a high degree of one or both can play the school game well and are labeled as "the smart ones." But kids wired by God with a high level of any of the other smarts are seen—by themselves and others—as square pegs trying to cram into round holes.

Homeschooling—whether embraced from a secular or faith-based perspective—was quite literally relaunched in the modern era as an alternative to what occurs in the schools.[3] The "modern pioneer" homeschoolers pulled their kids from the system in tacit protest of school culture; they intended to raise their children more holistically, focusing more on what mattered to the parents and on each child's uniqueness than what the system dictated.

And they did, at least at first. But I fear—based on what I've read and heard from some of those pioneering souls, as well as my own observations since I became involved in the homeschool community in 2005—that we're losing our saltiness, so to speak. Too many contemporary homeschoolers seem bent on replicating the school system in their homes. All loving parents obviously want their kids to be productive members of society, able to support their own families one day, but homeschooling parents don't need to imitate the trappings of the institutional school system that often requires all children to learn the same things, in the same ways, at the same rate.

Happily, homeschoolers don't have to elevate logic and word smart above the others. We have the freedom at home to fully honor how each of our kids has been designed—and then use our knowledge and love for our kids to activate, shape, and grow each one's complete strengths profile. Being holistic in that way will eventually enable them to confidently and unapologetically home in on careers in which they can excel and delight, even if word and logic smart are at the bottom of their proverbial lists.

When I covered language arts, I noted that creative writing is great but is not an essential life skill. That's true for all the fine arts. Your child can live a happy, fulfilled life even if she has no interest in cartooning or playing the oboe. But we risk robbing our kids of the chance to discover the full range of their abilities and smarts if we fail to provide and nurture opportunities to explore the fine arts. And we definitely owe it to them to support demonstrated skill in any of the arts. Indeed, we must acknowledge that some kids are actually *called* to fine arts–related careers or avocations.

Music Smart

I deduced that Rachel was probably music smart when she was three and demonstrated a natural ability to produce sustained tones on my French horn. I suspected Abbie's music smart at about the same age, when she joyfully belted out her favorite Bible songs—on pitch—using the portable karaoke toy she'd gotten for Christmas.

My husband hails from a highly music-smart family, and my in-laws begged us to enroll the girls in piano lessons. That was an easy request to honor; I'd have done it anyway, because I'm music smart and understand the foundational value of knowing piano. As it turns out, Rachel took lessons all through her school years and tackled an eleven-page Grieg solo her senior year. Abbie eventually switched from piano to voice and guitar, but her ability to play the piano proved invaluable to her other musical endeavors. In due time, both girls participated in our local homeschool choir and musical productions, where Abbie won several featured roles. To avoid overextending ourselves, we chose not to pursue wind instruments, but others in my town make the thirty-minute trek to a nearby community for homeschool band.

It's almost always possible to find a capable local piano teacher, and you may also have ready access to local instruction in other instruments via professional tutors or college music majors. But these days a local connection isn't even necessary, as you can secure instruction in almost any instrument via the internet. The Roadmap can help with that through its lists for Music: Instrumental Technique in the Deluxe Charts Project.

Look into community-based ensembles as well—such as boys' and girls' choirs, youth orchestras—or, if you can't find any, start your own. My friend Molly wanted her homeschooled kids to enjoy musical theater as she had growing up, so she started the homeschool musical theater program from which my girls and hundreds of other kids have benefitted over the years.

Picture Smart

In the section for Art in the Deluxe Charts Project, The Roadmap lists literally hundreds of curricular options in the visual arts—everything from crafting and painting for young children to sculpture, photography, and printmaking for teens. In our case, my husband, Jeff—a graphic artist by training—happily took the lead with art, coming up with myriad creative activities for the girls, both at home and on excursions around town. They fondly remember imitating ancient cave painters in Jeff's darkened base-ment office, drawing on brown paper bags with art pastels while using only the glow of candles for light, and sketching ducklings in a park during a weekend mini-vacation. But you don't have to be artistic yourself to offer such opportunities to your kids, as good programs provide step-by-step instructions. You might even inspire your kids and stretch your own smarts by learning right along with them.

You can also find community-based art instruction—my girls participated in a program taught by local professional art-ists and created many impressive projects—or ask an artistic parent in a homeschool group if she'd provide lessons. One of my friends offered art instruction to small groups of kids in her home; another currently holds classes at a local church. One year our homeschool group sponsored a visiting artist, Barry Steb-bing, who provided instruction to more than a hundred kids and parents for three full days.[4]

Nature Smart

The Charlotte Mason technique called "nature study" is a wonder-ful way to introduce the visual arts to a nature-smart child. Nature study requires only a sketchpad, a decent pencil, and maybe some colored pencils or watercolors. The child simply takes her supplies to a setting with plants, animals, or landscapes of interest—a botanical garden, hiking trail, or even your own backyard—settles in, and draws what she sees. The idea is to draw with care, aiming to produce accurate representations, perhaps in order to research various species back at home. A nature-smart kid will delight in such opportunities.

Exploring nature photography is another option. My husband still uses a fancy 35-mm camera, but most phones take impressive pictures with a bit of practice. For a teen with enough interest, you might also invest in formal instruction—online, through a local college or artists' group, or perhaps by having her shadow a willing professional photographer.

Body Smart

Like Kristin, body-smart kids—boys and girls—may be drawn to the art of dance. My girls took dance lessons from an early age, and Rachel performed a lyrical solo at her final recital. We used several studios along the way—everything from basic instruction at the YMCA to more concentrated study at a classical ballet school that sponsors one of my city's annual productions of *The Nutcracker*.

Dance was simply a hobby for my girls, but I personally know homeschoolers who have funneled their interest, gifts, and smarts into more serious study and even dance-related careers. Amelia, for example, studied intensely with classically trained ballerinas; as a result, she danced several featured roles in *The Nutcracker* while still in high school. Our dear friend Liliya discovered Irish dance at the age of nine and was able to regularly travel to competitions, where she excelled. She made it to the preliminary championship and was only one win away from making the open championship, the highest level of competition, before choosing to retire—with her parents' blessing—at seventeen. Another friend, Katelyn, has been the lead dance instructor at our local Kroc Center for several years and plans one day to open her own studio.

Word Smart

Word-smart kids enjoy the opportunity to participate in drama productions—with or without singing, depending on their music smart. While it's obviously possible to form a homeschool-specific troupe, it's also worth investigating community-based opportunities. My city has a children's theater company, Evergreen Productions, in which homeschooled kids regularly participate, often securing lead roles.

Speech and debate and forensics teams are other options for word-smart kids to try their hand in the arts. You can find or launch a local speech/debate club through the National Christian Forensics and Communications Association (NCFCA) or simply start your own, less formal group. For several years, my friend Amy led a monthly speech club wherein she offered basic instruction in public speaking and then encouraged the kids to take turns presenting speeches and dramatic readings to each other. As with Molly, her initial motivation was to provide an activity for her own children; in the process, she blessed many others.

Logic Smart

What about logic-smart kids—the analyzers and questioners? Depending on a logic-smart child's overall smarts profile, she may very well be interested in some or all of the aforementioned activities, especially debate. If not, though, consider that she may thrive behind the scenes, perhaps as a stage manager or production assistant.

During Rachel's junior year, Molly produced *Cinderella*. Rachel opted to volunteer for the stage crew rather than audition for a role, and she discovered her theater sweet spot in the process. Rachel is organized and detail-oriented, skills Molly quickly recognized and put to good use. In fact, knowing that Rachel was backstage—able and willing to keep track of scene changes, prop placement, and actor cues—relieved Molly of a great deal of pressure, allowing her to focus on the performers' singing, dancing, and acting. Rachel saw her natural abilities put to good use, and when she took an unexpected gap year right after high school she volunteered again to be Molly's assistant for a production of *Beauty and the Beast*.

Self Smart

Not surprisingly, self-smart kids opt for solitary fine arts–related activities, some if not all of the time. Though not through home-schooling, I had roles in a number of plays during my high school years and was a member of the pep and concert bands; I enjoyed making valuable contributions to those group efforts. But when given the option to work with a group or on my own, I always chose the latter. So I played solos at competitive music events, and I chose solo forensics categories instead of joining friends in their group endeavors. That was okay for me—and it's okay for your self-smart child. As long as a young person knows how to interact in social situations, there's nothing wrong with choosing to create art on her own.

People Smart

Group activities—choir, band, church worship team, dance companies, theater productions, speech teams, art classes—unquestionably provide natural forays into the arts for people-smart kids. In fact, choosing to become involved in arts-related group endeavors could provide just the right outlet to "save" homeschooling for your people-smart kid.

I've met a lot of homeschooled kids over the years—and heard about many more from their parents through online discussions. I know that some—probably the very people-smart kids—struggle with what they perceive to be the "isolation" of homeschooling. A kid like this idealizes "regular" school, begging to attend. No doubt a grass-is-always-greener mentality comes into play here, and the homeschooled child doesn't realize how often schoolteachers have to admonish students in class to "stop socializing!" But it can be hard as a parent to say no (if enrolling your child in conventional school is not in keeping with your personal convictions) without breaking that child's spirit.

Intentionally chosen, regularly scheduled activities can go a long way toward meeting a people-smart child's real needs for interaction beyond the family.

I don't believe homeschooling parents should run themselves ragged, scheduling myriad extracurriculars every day; part of homeschooling is, after all, about the safe haven of home itself. However, intentionally chosen, regularly scheduled activities to which your people-smart child can look forward can go a long way toward meeting her real needs for interaction beyond the family. Why not activate and develop her interest in the fine arts in the process?

Providing Opportunities

The fine arts are elective—optional. If a child gives dance, drama, art, and/or music a solid try but ultimately lacks enough interest to sustain the effort, it's okay to put the activity on a shelf. Once exposed, she'll know it's there and may take it up later in life. Just be sure to provide opportunities for exposure to those beautiful endeavors.

Can you think of something to consider right now for each of your kids? Make a note in your smarts journal.

ELECTIVES:
The Sky's the
LIMIT

When people hear the word "electives," most automatically and understandably think about high school and transcripts.[1] Prior to when our kids reach the high school level, we might think about whether we're addressing "core" content—that is, math, language arts, science, and social studies (occasionally fine arts or health, depending on a state's homeschool law)—or "something else," and we may consider in general terms how various broad content areas fit within the parameters of the law. But it's not usually until we reach the point of awarding credits and making transcripts that we officially think about electives.

Because of this, you will probably think mostly in terms of high school throughout this chapter. That's appropriate, but younger kids can delve into "elective" areas as well, even if we don't slap official labels onto what they're learning. We do our young kids a great service by allowing them to explore all sorts of content beyond the "big four" as their interests and passions dictate. In fact, giving our younger kids room to explore electives comes with a host of benefits: making some of the "core" subjects more tolerable, vastly enriching their overall learning experiences, giving them direction about what to pursue in a more in-depth way during high school, and beginning to reveal career paths God may have designed for them.

We do our young kids a great service by allowing them to explore all sorts of content as their interests and passions dictate.

The beautiful thing about electives at any age is that they are—elective! They're optional. In contrast to "core" content, instruction in electives isn't mandatory. For that reason, we can treat them differently than we do the "core."

With core content—especially the "big four"—we think about required knowledge and skills (for example, that every child should know how to add and subtract, comprehend written text, communicate clearly, etc.), and we can use a child's smarts profile to maximize his learning and retention. In other words, the content is rather static, but the delivery methods vary, kid by kid. With electives, though, the content itself is variable.

Some kids—based on their smarts, personal interests, and

future plans—may want to study accounting; others desire to learn French, interior design, or robotics. Any of that content—and much more—can legitimately be incorporated into a homeschool child's learning endeavors (at any age), but none is necessary for every child. Thus, we have the great blessing to completely personalize everything beyond the bare bones of the "core" to suit how each child has been intrinsically wired, deciding on delivery methods *and* the content itself based on each one's smarts profiles.

As I developed The Homeschool Resource Roadmap and then again when my girls entered their high school years, I took note of the various categories of elective content offered by curriculum providers and studied typical transcript course titles. From that research, I've been able to comprehend the broad spectrum of elective possibilities, and I see how it's possible to classify the various options by smart.

Picture Smart

I discussed fine arts as its own category in the previous chapter because homeschool laws in some states mandate the inclusion of the arts as part of home-based educational programs. Those states generally give parents broad discretion in addressing the law's requirements—for instance, a picture-smart child can focus on the visual arts while a music-smart kid can emphasize learning to play an instrument. But under most state homeschool laws, the arts as a whole are considered elective, giving you even more leeway to customize.

Not surprisingly, a picture-smart kid will undoubtedly be drawn to electives related to the visual arts—art history, drawing, filmmaking, graphic design, painting, photography, printmaking, and sculpture. He may dabble in several, earning a half or whole credit in each. Or he may home in on one, accruing multiple credits—demonstrating beginning, intermediate, and advanced skill—in one particular area of passion.[2]

But other elective areas that facilitate visualization of an end-product are also likely to be of interest. For example, picture-smart kids may resonate with creative writing, where they can "paint pictures" with words. They may enjoy what I categorize as Home Management areas on The Roadmap (automotive repair, cosmetology, culinary arts, interior design, home repair, metallurgy, sewing, embroidery, knitting, quilting, crocheting, fashion design, and woodworking) or what I label as Technology (AutoCAD, engineering, coding and computer programming, drafting, architecture, electronics, robotics, digital game design, and web design). All of the these require an ability to make mental pictures of both the process and end-product, a definite strength for picture-smart learners.

Music Smart

It goes without saying that music-smart kids will be drawn to elective work in which they can study and/or make music. We think first in this regard of mastering the techniques for playing musical instruments—any instrument in the brass, strings, woodwind, or percussion families; fretted instruments such as guitar, bass, banjo, mandolin, or ukulele; the piano or organ; more esoteric options such as harmonica, ocarina, tin whistle, harp, or hand bells; or even something as basic as the recorder or ubiquitous as voice. A child may try out several possibilities (Abbie learned piano, voice, and both the acoustic and classical guitar) or stick with one for many years the way Rachel did.

But music-smart kids can study music history, theory, and composition as well, earning credit for their time and effort. My girls' friend Rose plays many instruments and took paying jobs as a wedding pianist and church organist and pianist while still in high school. She also wrote her own music compositions. Our friends Drew and Elizabeth formed a band shortly before they married, turning their individual homeschool music studies into a fulfilling endeavor. They write their own songs and sing and play multiple instruments at coffee houses and local festivals.

Interestingly, some music-smart kids may also show interest in learning a foreign language. While at first glance that sounds incongruous, it really does make sense because music-smart people think in melodies and rhythms. Thus, the cadence of languages—particularly the more lyrical ones—can seem mellifluous to music-smart learners' ears.

Word Smart

I mentioned in the chapters on language arts and fine arts that word-smart kids are apt to be drawn to creative writing—and, because being able to write fiction and poetry is not a "life skill," time spent in such endeavors can be considered elective. In addition, word-smart kids may show interest in elective subjects that emphasize reading—art history, music history, the history of science or the Bible, anthropology, health and wellness, cultural studies, region-specific literary analysis (such as Brit Lit or Early American Literature), criminology, philosophy, psychology—as long as you provide engaging, well-written material.

Because a word-smart kid likes "playing with words," he may also enjoy studying a foreign language (of which The Roadmap lists more than a hundred possibilities). Or, if he shares his writing via a blog, he may choose to dabble in web design as well. He may be interested in a speed-reading course. And, though all kids should learn keyboarding, a word-smart kid may demonstrate more motivation to gain mastery than others, if for no other reason than that it will facilitate his writing process.

Body Smart

So many elective options exist for body-smart kids! In fact, though much of the content found in "the core four"—particularly if delivered in conventional, school-style ways—might frustrate body-smart learners, many electives seem built for them.

Those who are body- *and* picture-smart will dive into the visual arts that actually involve making projects—that is, everything except, perhaps, art history. Likewise, they may resonate with most of the same Home Management- and Technology-oriented electives of interest to picture-smart kids, because those endeavors require tactile involvement and physical movement.

A body-smart kid might easily and happily rack up credits in physical education too, perhaps even completing distinct courses of study in several fitness endeavors—one credit in weight-lifting, another in racket sports, yet another in cardio-training. He may also show interest in taking a first-aid course. And he's apt to excel in keyboarding and driver education, another basic teen rite of passage which can legitimately be listed as a transcript elective.

In terms of more traditionally "academic" electives, consider introducing your body-smart kid to STEM and archaeology material. STEM coursework is, by design, very hands-on. Archaeology can be as well, particularly if you can find ways to incorporate actual "digs" of some sort rather than simply having the child read books and watch videos.

Nature Smart

A nature-smart learner might take up some of the visual arts—drawing, filmmaking, painting, and photography—if he's allowed to focus on outdoor-oriented themes. He may also show serious interest in sculpture, particularly if he can make his own clay and/or use a variety of natural materials in his creations. The same holds true for areas such as metallurgy, woodworking, and the textile arts, since all involve the use of natural materials.

Elective sciences such as astronomy, the earth sciences (environmental science, geology, meteorology), and advanced biology (agriscience, botany, forestry, horticulture, zoology, veterinary science, human anatomy and physiology) hold appeal for nature-smart kids, as does archaeology if—as with body-smart learners—they are allowed to actually participate in digs. It's even possible to turn nature-based hobbies and interests into legitimate elective coursework. For example, a teen who volunteers at a horse farm in exchange for riding lessons can translate what he's learned into a credit of equestrian science. Or you may help a kid who loves fishing design an in-depth unit study (i.e., learning about various freshwater fish and their habitats, etc.) that can become a bona fide transcript course.

Logic Smart

Content that requires analysis and problem-solving appeals to logic-smart kids. Thus, elective math-oriented coursework—accounting, personal finance, pre-calculus, trigonometry, calculus, and statistics—will resonate, as will technology-based subjects such as coding/computer programming, digital game design, and web design. A logic-smart learner will also gravitate toward forensics, criminology, and STEM, all of which lend themselves to the asking and answering of questions. He may fall in love with anthropology and archaeology, which involve trying to solve the mysteries of the past.

This type of learner may also enjoy architecture and interior design, which require the ability to solve design problems. He may find delight in an experimental culinary arts course that lets him investigate how various ingredients work together to create new and interesting dishes.

Finally, some logic-smart learners love studying foreign languages, viewing their structure and grammar as problems to solve in comparison to that of their native language. "Logical" languages—the ones, like Spanish, which are largely "regular" in construction—will appeal more than languages (like English!) where the rules are broken more often than not.

Self Smart

Areas that directly apply to a self-smart learner's life will have the most direct appeal for him. So a self-smart kid may take a deep interest in health and wellness, first aid, psychology, and personal finance. He will value the opportunity to earn physical education credit in solitary endeavors—such as working one-on-one with a trainer at a gym—rather than group classes. And he may look forward to driver education as an opportunity to grow his personal independence.

If he's also music-smart, he'll seek to earn credit in solo-oriented instruments—such as piano or guitar—rather than options more suited for group performance. And if he's also word-smart, you can help him design a course in Personal Memoir, allowing him to read various autobiographical works and then also write his own memoir.

A self-smart kid may have a particular interest in entrepreneurship, in being his own boss. And almost any of the Art-, Home Management-, and/or Technology-related electives already mentioned can suit a self-smart learner well because they can be undertaken individually. For example, a self-smart teen might combine his study of how to launch his own business with his interest in carpentry to open his own woodworking shop in your garage, concurrently earning high school credit and real-world job experience.

People Smart

People-smart kids may have an interest in entrepreneurship and marketing as well, but with an eye toward working with others in the business world. The musically inclined will gravitate toward instruments that generally fit well within bands and orchestras or will pursue voice instruction and participation in choirs. When earning physical education credits, they'll prefer to participate in group fitness classes.

Once a child's basic learning needs are met, you can use elective content in ways that maximize each child's demonstrated passions and talents.

Because people-smart learners enjoy putting themselves in others' shoes, they may fancy art and music history and region-specific literary analysis. And they'll likely resonate with elective social studies coursework such as criminology, psychology, sociology, and cross-cultural studies (for example, Latin American history or Asian studies), as well as child development, anthropology, and hospitality and tourism. They may also dive headfirst into mastering a foreign language or two as a purposeful stepping-stone toward eventually traveling the world to meet new people and experience different cultures.

Unlimited Horizons

The sky really is the limit when it comes to elective coursework for our homeschooled kids. Once a child's basic learning needs are met, you can use elective content in ways that maximize each child's demonstrated passions and talents. Even if your kids are young—and especially if they're in or approaching their high school years—take time now to jot down some ideas that have stood out to you and any other possibilities that came to mind. Then ask your kids—particularly your tweens and teens—what they'd like to learn about and begin figuring how to turn their ideas into documentable electives.

RELIGIOUS EDUCATION:
WORSHIPFUL
Accommodation

M omma, I wanna pray to let Jesus into my heart."
It was September 1, 2006, and we were in the middle
of breakfast. As I recall, we had not been having a spiritually
oriented discussion, but five-year-old Rachel nonetheless made
this sudden pronouncement. I hesitated. I definitely wanted
both girls to make personal professions of faith, but Rachel was
so young, and this was completely out of the blue. Did she really
know what she was saying? Would any prayer to receive Christ
"stick" in her barely-out-of-toddlerhood mind?

I sensed I should honor rather than question her desire. I
ushered her into the hallway—leaving Abbie and a little girl I'd
been babysitting to chat with each other—and pulled her onto my
lap. We talked for a few minutes about her interest in accepting

Jesus' salvation gift, and it really did seem sincere and Spirit-led. I knew she'd have to mature in her faith as she grew physically and cognitively, but I felt comfortable leading her in a simple prayer acknowledging her need for Jesus to be her Savior and Lord.

I had decided to begin living my life as a follower of Jesus while in college. My husband and I committed to raising our children on that foundation before we ever married, hoping to help them acknowledge and embrace John 14:6—that Jesus is the way and the truth and the life, and that no one comes to God the Father except through Him. We've approached parenting through the lens of that particular worldview perspective.

Worldview is, in fact, everything.

"A worldview is a theory of the world, used for living in the world. A worldview is a mental model of reality—a framework of ideas [and] attitudes about the world, ourselves, and life, a comprehensive system of beliefs—with answers for a wide range of questions."[1] Every person comes at life from a particular worldview perspective.

We often hold at least parts of a worldview subconsciously, but that view nevertheless affects everything we say and do in one way or another. And, whether that view is based on one religion or another or is, instead, secular, it's actually impossible for any human being to approach life from a wholly objective perspective. We aren't robots; to be human means to take a position about how the world operates.

So you will unavoidably teach and train your kids from the basis of your worldview, whatever it is. Teach tolerance for all perspectives, but don't attempt the impossible task of parenting from a worldview-neutral perspective. You—not someone else on the planet—have been given your particular kids for a slew of reasons, among them the gift and responsibility of (graciously but unapologetically) imparting your specific beliefs and values to them as you see fit. Take up that mantle with confidence.

In terms of homeschooling, some choose to include religious education as a specific stand-alone subject, alongside language arts and math and art. Others see such instruction as worldview training that undergirds, overarches, and infuses every part of each day of their lives with their kids, such that it's always "there" as a presence in their homes even when it doesn't show up as a distinct item on a lesson plan. I fall into the latter camp, which is why I've chosen to address "religious education" as a distinct topic rather than as one of many possible elective courses of study and why I've saved discussing it till now. But, in either case, it's certainly a good idea to utilize a child's smarts strengths to help her learn, retain, and personally adopt the worldview position you teach and model—whether it's similar to mine or something entirely different.

People Smart

We raised both our daughters in the same environment, aiming to consistently impart a biblical worldview, and Rachel "prayed the prayer" at five. Abbie, on the other hand, will tell you she didn't make a personal commitment to Christ until July 15, 2015, when she was thirteen years old.

Abbie listened to all the stories from the two excellent Bible storybooks we used when the girls were young.[2] She memorized verses and learned Scripture songs. She attended Sunday school and VBS and was just as excited as Rachel to start coming to "big church." Always willing to please and rather calm by nature, she seemingly exhibited the fruit of the Spirit rather consistently. But it wasn't until she attended a summer Bible camp that she actually gave herself to Christ.

God gives us the responsibility to be our kids' primary instructors, in spiritual matters and everything else.

I believe that's in part due to Abbie's people-smart strength. She learns well with other people, so it makes sense that the Holy Spirit could impact her in a significant way as she lived and studied Scripture with a couple of hundred other youth. She needed the affirmation of being with a large group of like-minded people.

As homeschoolers, we like to be in control of what our kids learn and experience; indeed, God gives us the responsibility to be their primary instructors, in spiritual matters and everything else. But He's also wired our people-smart kids to need people—likely beyond our own families—to most effectively think and learn. So be open to the possibility that, though the Lord will use you to plant and water seeds in your people-smart child's life, He may orchestrate someone else to bring in the harvest.

Keep in mind that people-smart kids may be more apt than others to adopt the views of those with whom they spend time. As such, you may have to exercise care and wisdom in choosing group experiences for them. But it's healthy to provide opportunities for people-smart children and teens to foster spiritual growth in appropriate group settings. Our family had been involved with the camp where Abbie made her profession of faith for nine years before she actually attended on her own, so we were confident about the fellowship and instruction she received.

Self Smart

My personal testimony involves God pursuing me for several months when I was a college freshman. He used the witness of new friends on campus, the pastor and evangelism team from a local church, and a former teacher in my hometown. When I finally put all the pieces together and realized God was actively seeking me, I did what any self-respecting self-smart person would do: I went home, closed myself up in my bedroom, and talked to Him about it all on my own. Afterward, I didn't announce my conversion; I simply started showing up to InterVarsity meetings and bumming rides to church, letting my actions speak for my new-found faith commitment.

You may find yourself concerned about your self-smart child's faith because she keeps it largely to herself and may balk about attending Sunday school or youth group. After all, self-smart kids process and learn best when they're alone, given time and space to reflect. Thus, you may need to exercise your own faith in regard to your self-smart child, trusting that God's got hold of her even when you're not sure! But you can facilitate the spiritual development of a self-smart child by making high-quality content and materials—devotional books and study guides, concordances and study Bibles, subscriptions to Bible-teaching podcasts, journaling tools, etc.—readily available.

Another good tool for helping self-smart children grow is the spiritual dialogue journal. Simply designate a particular notebook and ask a self-smart kid to spend a bit of time writing you a letter about spiritual ideas or questions that currently interest her. Direct her to fill at least one side of one page, if possible, and more if she'd like. Then read what she's said and write back in response, not as an evaluator but as a fellow pilgrim on the road. Assign her one letter each week and be faithful in responding promptly so she has time to process her next reply. Keep this going—focused specifically on faith-related matters—over time. You'll be amazed at her insight, and you'll be creating a keepsake of her spiritual growth at the same time.

Music Smart

My dear friend Denise—the mom of Irish dancer Liliya—cracks me up. Upon moving to a new community, she and her family began hunting for a new church home. After each visit, she reported their initial impressions to me. On more than one occasion, she matter-of-factly declared her lack of interest in a church because "they did too much singing!"

Music-smart isn't one of Denise's top strengths so, though she understands the value of worshipping through song, she prefers it in small doses. I, on the other hand, learn through music and could sing for a full hour or more before the start of a sermon!

You may find a similar contrast among your kids, depending on the level of music smart with which each has been designed. A music-smart child will resonate with Scripture memory songs, serenade you with the VBS theme song for weeks on end, benefit from listening to spiritual music in the background at home, and may hope to serve on your church's worship team in due time. Some music-smart kids even try their hand at composing their own worship songs.

Remembering that music-smart learners actually learn

through music, you can also use this strength to help them develop a solid biblical theology. Contemporary worship songs may work for this to some degree, but hymns—whether or not they're sung in your church—generally carry more theological weight. So, borrow a hymnal from your church or research and purchase one whose song selection comports with your faith perspective.

As with every area of the homeschool life, it's perfectly acceptable and totally normal to learn right alongside your kids in regard to spiritual matters.

Then encourage your music-smart child to use it. She might learn to play and/or sing various hymns, but also challenge her to study the lyrics in their own right and use a concordance to dig into related Bible verses.

Word Smart

Related to her word-smart strength, one thing Denise cannot do without is solid, expository preaching of the Word. While we should all desire to grow in our love for strong biblical instruction, word-smart learners crave it—if presented clearly in an engaging manner.

Your word-smart child may enjoy the spiritual dialogue journal idea I mentioned above. In addition, remember that word-smart people process and learn via talking, so be sure to make time to let her talk with you about devotional readings, personal Bible study,

Sunday school and youth group lessons, and sermons. You don't need to be a spiritual giant to do this! As with every area of the homeschool life, it's perfectly acceptable and totally normal to learn right alongside your kids in regard to spiritual matters.

In our home, I didn't want "Bible" to feel like just another school subject, so we did our devotional time over breakfast, before we jumped into bookwork, and I avoided setting time limits. We usually engaged in meaningful discussions for a reasonable amount of time and then moved on. Sometimes, however, one point led to another and another and yet another—all of which were relevant—and an hour or more (occasionally much more) passed before we knew it! Thinking about the time these spiritual rabbit trails consumed sometimes made me anxious—and certainly if a child attempts to use tangents to avoid working on other content or if the family has a scheduled activity to attend later in the day, time should be taken into consideration—but I inevitably saw the greater good. Academics are important, but if I wanted to demonstrate to my kids that things of God really are the foundation upon which I hoped they'd build their lives, I had to prioritize pertinent discussion related to Him.

Logic Smart

Logic-smart kids sometimes struggle with faith. They are, after all, wired to ask questions and seek satisfying answers. We can certainly harness that strength to encourage in-depth Bible study, as well as the study of works by serious apologists like C. S. Lewis and Francis Schaeffer and once-skeptical scientists and philosophers who eventually came to faith.

But some matters of faith aren't fully knowable in this life—we are, after all, called to "walk by faith, not by sight" (2 Cor. 5:7)—and logic-smart learners may have a hard time accepting that. If you're parenting a highly logic-smart child, choose to be gracious with—not judgmental of—her. She may very well want to believe even as her struggle to do so is genuinely real (Mark 9:24).

Many people tacitly believe God provides one of three answers to prayer: *yes, no,* and *maybe,* an idea which probably stems from parents' responses to their kids' various requests. But that's not biblically accurate. God's actual answers are *yes, no,* and *not yet.*

Pray like crazy, seek discernment about when to speak and when to listen, and trust. God loves your child even more than you do.

Teaching a logic-smart child this truth may go a long way toward easing her apprehension about her unanswerable questions. It's not that God *might* one day answer, if He feels like it. That view turns the Lord into a fickle tyrant. Rather, teach your child that she's promised eventual answers—perhaps later in this life or definitely in eternity—even when she can't know now.

At root, logic-smart learners don't want easy-believe-ism. Thus, you may need to back off and let God do His thing, even if it takes time. Pray like crazy, seek discernment about when to speak and when to listen, and trust. God loves your child even more than you do; He doesn't fear her questions and doubt.

Nature Smart

If you're like me, you may have laughed—or rolled your eyes—when someone has declared that she "worships God better in the woods than in church." That seems like an excuse to sleep in on Sunday mornings—and it might be. But what if it isn't?

Nature-smart people actually do learn well outside, as they encounter the beauty and structure of the natural world. And, if they acknowledge the Creator who designed what they see, isn't it possible that they actually do worship Him more readily in the midst of that creation than while primly sitting in church pews?

I'm not suggesting we allow our nature-smart kids to skip church services; at the very least, attending church allows them to "not neglect meeting" with other believers (Heb. 10:25), and that's important. But if we truly want a child to grow spiritually, we should work with how she's wired instead of dismissing her. So instead of badgering a nature-smart kid for not listening in church, compliment her for attending without complaining. Then set her up with an audio sermon—from your church or another reputable source—and let her take that walk in the woods. Encourage her to pray as she walks and stop somewhere to journal. Talk with her when she returns—focusing specifically on spiritual insights she gained. Let her do "nature church" at least once a week along with attending indoor services.

Body Smart

Many of us have unconsciously accepted a cultural norm that says that "sitting still" when doing "spiritual things" is respectful. Yet body-smart people actually learn better when they move. So sitting still in Sunday school or church—or during family devotions—is tough on them. They struggle to focus and are often shamed for being disrespectful if they squirm. But a body-smart child can learn to channel her need for movement in appropriate ways to actually facilitate her spiritual growth.

For example, she can color or draw or even work on a puzzle or build (quietly) with Legos during family Bible study. Doing so in Sunday school would distract other kids, but she can draw and color—or work on dot-to-dot books—in a church service without distracting. So allowing a body-smart child to attend "big church" with her "learning tools" rather than a children's service might (counterintuitively) be one of the best things you can do for her.

As body-smart kids get older, they can learn to take notes as a way to focus during sermons and family devotionals. But allowing them to move in other ways is still appropriate as well. Rachel knits and crochets during our pastors' sermons and reports that doing so increases her ability to pay attention.

Picture Smart

Coloring or drawing during sermons and spiritual discussions also works well with picture-smart learners of all ages. In fact, a woman at a church I used to attend—a doctor and a homeschooling mom—used high-quality charcoal pencils to sketch elaborate biblical scenes from her regular seat near the front of the church during sermons. Her work fascinated those near her but didn't bother anyone else, and drawing helped her focus and remember key points.

In terms of family study, at least two picture-smart Bible study programs—*The Picture-Smart Bible*, which is owned and marketed by Kathy Koch and Celebrate Kids, and *Grapevine Studies*—exist to help us along. Both programs are built on the use of simple illustrations to help learners (of all ages) retain and apply biblical truth. Both can serve well as a means of engaging your picture-smart kids in Bible study, as well as growing family relationships and supporting the development of every family member's picture smart.

A Creative Act of Worship

Some of these teaching ideas may seem disrespectful or radical at first glance. But if you believe your faith or worldview perspective anchors the rest of your home-learning endeavors, you'll want to do whatever will effectively impart your spiritual values to your kids. In fact, you may want to read the section on Spiritual Growth Kathy has included in each chapter of *8 Great Smarts* for even more ideas.[3]

God didn't make any mistakes when He wired your kids as He has, so you can embrace the truth that your attempt to match spiritual learning to their smarts profiles isn't lazy or rude. Accommodating how the Lord has designed your kids as you help them learn about Him is actually an act of worship on your part.

The
BOTTOM Line

Homeschoolers—even those new to the lifestyle—know the most common question we're asked by outsiders is some iteration of, "But what about socialization?" Thankfully, we learn rather quickly to shake our heads and laugh that off (if people only understood all the opportunities with which our kids are blessed!). But we have our own in-house question, which is just as insignificant in the grand scheme: "What curriculum do you use?"

Gather two or more homeschoolers in a room, and it won't be long before this question is asked—and then thoroughly hashed out. And I get it. Learning what other parents use to educate their kids is a way to build camaraderie and community—our very own special, secret handshake. And homeschooling parents are incredibly conscientious. We want to hear what others use in case someone knows of a curriculum that's "better." We're game for whatever it might take—including making curriculum changes—to do right by our kids.

Our diligence is commendable. I know from my research that we have literally thousands of resource options from which to choose—not to mention material we create on our own![1] So though there's literally no such thing as a perfect curriculum, seeking a very good fit for each of our kids is a real part of our job as home-educators. In fact, I've sought to show you various practical ways for using your understanding of your kids' smarts profiles—applied to whatever curriculum you choose—to strengthen each one's overall educational experience.

What you need most of all to succeed as a home-educating parent is a desire to grow and maintain abiding relationships with each of your kids.

But owning excellent learning tools—textbooks, workbooks, videos, project kits, etc.—isn't the key to successful homeschooling. Nor is aiming for the impossible goal of attaining personal mastery over every bit of content you think your kids might one day need to know. In fact, the lynchpin isn't even having a thorough intellectual understanding of how God has wired your kids' brains.

What you need most of all to succeed as a home-educating parent is a desire to grow and maintain abiding relationships with each of your kids. And an aspiration as lofty as that springs only from a place of deep, unconditional love.

If you're partly motivated to homeschool out of obedience to God's calling, your deference to Him is ultimately a demonstration of your love for Him (John 14:21). That love should be the starting place in all things for any Christ-follower. And God will bless your obedience with ultimate success—as He has ordained—in the lives of each of your kids (Prov. 22:6).

Obligation, stress, and anxiety sometimes conspire to block our view of the very love that drew us to keep our kids home in the first place.

I also know without having met you that you deeply love your kids. Your dedication to doing all it takes to own the responsibility for your kids' academic learning in addition to the rest of their well-being speaks for itself. But sometimes in the midst of a long-term commitment, we lose sight of the forest for the trees. We can get caught up in the pressure—of finding materials, making time to fit it all in every day, maximizing each child's potential, keeping skeptics at bay, battling our kids' attitude problems . . . and our own. We don't ever stop loving our kids, but obligation, stress, and anxiety sometimes conspire to block our view of the very love that drew us to keep our kids home in the first place.

Think of driving your car through a summer rainstorm. You

begin your journey on a bright, sunny day with a clear vision of the road ahead and miles of vista all around. But clouds roll in and fat droplets plink onto your windshield with increasing fervor. You can still see, but you click on your wipers, initially using the intermittent setting. Then you pass under a billowing dark cloud bank that dumps its full force of moisture onto the vehicle. You crank up the wipers, stretch out your neck, and squint to keep just a few feet of the ribbon of road in view. The downpour keeps coming, throwing sheets of water at you, until the wipers are on their highest setting—whipping back and forth, back and forth. You slow down. You're not quite sure where the road is anymore. Finally, you pull over, afraid to keep going, and turn off the wipers to avoid burning out the motor. As the deluge rages, you eventually lose sight of the road. You know it's there—able to help you reach your destination—because roads once set in place don't actually vanish, but you can't see it.

Love is what will carry you to your desired destination.

Thank goodness every storm eventually clears. The sun bursts forth again, and you're able to pull back out and continue the journey.

Homeschool life is like weather, complete with occasional but regular bouts of rain—sometimes in drizzles, other times in full-force thunderstorms. Your family is the car, and the tools of the homeschool trade—curriculum, knowledge of the smarts, etc.—are the wipers. Love is the road.

Love is there even when you can't see it. Love is what will carry you to your desired destination. Through all the inevitable difficulty of driving through—and sometimes pulling over in the midst of—the storms of homeschool life, your main job is to keep sight of the love—and to choose to remember it's there even if it's sometimes blurred beyond recognition.

Your love for your kids—that Momma (or Papa) Bear instinct God has infused into every cell of your being—fuels your desire to build relationships with them. You can then harness solid relationships to help you manage through the ups and downs of homeschool life, working together with your kids to find good resources and discover the best ways to engage each of their smarts. Kids respond—maybe not instantly or perfectly, but they do respond—when their parents engage with them from a place of love.

As I mentioned before, neither of my girls has a love affair with math. I kept each one's smarts in mind when aiming to help them learn important mathematical concepts, and I tried a handful of curricular options through the years. But I knew if we were going to encounter a stress-point on any given day, the trigger would more than likely be math.

I wish I could say I always handled a math-related meltdown perfectly. I can't. But I can tell you that angst dissipated much more quickly and lessons proceeded more smoothly when I responded from a place of love, prioritizing my relationships with the girls over math facts. I learned that taking a few minutes to hold a math-stressed little girl—or, when she was older, to lead her by the hand away from the math book and let her sit on the couch with her head on my shoulder—made a world of difference. Long division and quadratic equations could wait. And they seemed a lot less daunting after a few minutes spent in the arms of the lady who—along with my husband—loves them wholeheartedly.

If you lose track of the truth that love is the bottom line, your relationships with your kids will suffer. Either you won't have the patience for them or they won't for you. If that happens, the fanciest, most expensive curriculum on the market won't help. You'll rail against them for "wasting all that money," and they'll resent you for valuing school over them. Even aiming to tailor activities toward their smarts won't matter without love—because without love you'll lose motivation to customize for your kids in the first place. The storms will seem permanent, not fleeting, and continuing on the journey will feel pointless.

I'm privileged to know two modern homeschooling pioneers—two more Titus 2 women in my life—who've inspired me to keep love at the forefront of my mind each and every day. I met Bobbie Howard in 2008 through an online homeschool support group she had joined to encourage us young moms. I later read her book *Encouragement Along the Way*.[2] I first got to know Karen

Campbell through her stellar book, *The Joy of Relationship Home-schooling*,[3] and eventually connected with her online. These ladies homeschooled their children when it was a "new thing" back in the '70s and '80s. Their kids then homeschooled their own children, and now the grandchildren are marrying and starting their own families, hopefully with the intent to homeschool. What a legacy!

Karen and Bobbie desired for each of their kids to be intellectually competent, physically and emotionally healthy, and spiritually grounded. They worked hard to ensure that each child was prepared to launch well into adult life, both for the kids' well-being and as an act of worship to God. But they prioritized love-planted relationship with each of their kids. All the rest of their respective homeschool journeys grew from that foundation of love. That's why each woman has a testimony to younger home-schooling parents. That's why each family has a multi-generational homeschool history.

As The Mom Psychologist, Dr. Jazmine McCoy, says, "In a world of hurry, fear, and competition, I am here to tell you [that] raising successful children has more to do with our presence than it has to do with racing them to the next 'enrichment' activity or helping them memorize flash cards. Arguably the single best thing you can do for your children's minds and emotional development is to simply enjoy your relationship with them."[4]

Perhaps the best way to sum up the bottom line—the place

from which your skill as a homeschooling parent and your ability to apply the eight great smarts to your kids' lives will blossom—is to quote the unknown author of this rendition of 1 Corinthians 13, written specifically for homeschooling parents. This has been floating around the internet since at least 2007, never (unfortunately) with an attributable source, but it's brilliant and, thus, worth sharing:

> If I teach my children how to multiply, divide, and diagram a
> sentence, but fail to show them love, I have taught them nothing.
> If I take them on numerous field trips, to swim practice, and flute
> lessons, and if I involve them in every church activity, but fail
> to give them love, I will profit nothing. And if I scrub my house
> relentlessly, run countless errands, and serve three nutritious meals
> every day but fail to be an example of love, I have done nothing.
>
> Love is patient with misspelled words and is kind to young
> interrupters. Love does not envy the high SAT scores of other
> homeschool families. Love does not claim to have better teaching
> methods than anyone else, is not rude to the fourth telephone caller
> during a science lesson, does not seek perfectly behaved geniuses,
> does not turn into a drill sergeant, thinks no evil about friends' edu-
> cational choices. Love bears all my children's challenges, believes all
> my children are God's precious gifts, hopes all my children establish
> permanent relationships with Christ, and endures all things . . .

Where there are college degrees, they will fail; where there is knowledge, it will vanish away. For we know in part and we teach in part. But when the trials of life come to our children, the history, math, and science will be done away, and faith, hope, and love will remain. But the greatest of these is love.

May God "bless you and keep you" on your family's homeschool journey. May He "make his face shine upon you and be gracious to you . . . and give you peace" along the way (Num. 6:24–26). You have a great "cloud of [homeschool] witnesses" (Heb. 12:1)—both recently and throughout most of human history in every culture—who've gone before, testifying through the lives of their kids and grandkids that it can be done. Gather good tools, be prepared to persevere, and go in love.

Love never fails.

APPENDIX

The Deluxe Charts Project is the most comprehensive section of The Homeschool Resource Roadmap (www.homeschoolroadmap.org). For those seeking to find good learning material for their kids, it's the most useful part of the site to study and bookmark. It categorizes every resource provider by subject area and then charts a number of features for each one. Curricular options exist in all of the following subject areas:

AGES 5-18

MULTI-SUBJECT PACKAGES

- Traditional/School-Style
  - Online/Video
  - Print-Based
- Unit Studies
  - Bible-Based
  - Geography-Based
  - History-Based
  - Literature-Based
  - Math-Based
  - Music-Based
  - Science-Based
  - Thematic
- Other Approaches
  - Charlotte Mason/Living Books
  - Classical

- *Guided Unschooling*
- *Montessori/Reggio/Waldorf*
- *Principle Approach*
- *Thomas Jefferson Education*
- *Project-Based Learning*

INDIVIDUAL SUBJECTS

Art
- Appreciation/History
  - *Crafting*
  - *Drawing/Illustration*
  - *Filmmaking*
  - *Graphic Design*
  - *Painting*
  - *Photography*
  - *Printmaking*
  - *Sculpture/Ceramics*

Business Education
- Accounting/Business Math
- Entrepreneurship
- Keyboarding
- Marketing
- Office Skills

Foreign Language
- Africa
  - *Afrikaans*
  - *Amharic*
  - *Chichewa (Chewa)*
  - *Hausa*
  - *Igbo*
  - *Malagasy*
  - *Oromo*
  - *Shona*
  - *Somali*
  - *Swahili*
  - *Tswana*
  - *Twi*
  - *Xhosa*
  - *Yoruba*
  - *Zulu*
  - *Other*
- Asia
  - *Bengali*
  - *Burmese*
  - *Cambodian*
  - *Cebuano*
  - *Chinese*
  - *Hindi*
  - *Hmong*
  - *Indonesian*
  - *Japanese*
  - *Korean*
  - *Lao*
  - *Malay*
  - *Malayalam*
  - *Marathi*
  - *Mongolian*
  - *Nepali*
  - *Punjabi*
  - *Sinhala*
  - *Tagalog (Filipino)*
  - *Tamil*
  - *Telugu*
  - *Thai*
  - *Tibetan*

- Vietnamese
- Other
- Europe
  - Albanian
  - Armenian
  - Basque
  - Belarusian
  - Bosnian
  - Bulgarian
  - Catalan
  - Cornish
  - Croatian
  - Czech
  - Danish
  - Dutch
  - Estonian
  - Finnish
  - French
  - Galician
  - Georgian
  - German
  - Greek
  - Hungarian
  - Icelandic
  - Irish
  - Italian
  - Latvian
  - Lithuanian
  - Luxembourgish
  - Macedonian
  - Maltese
  - Norwegian
  - Polish
  - Portuguese
  - Romanian
  - Russian
  - Scottish
  - Serbian
  - Slovak
  - Slovene/Slovenian
  - Swedish
  - Ukrainian
  - Welsh
  - Other
- Middle East
  - Arabic
  - Azerbaijani
  - Dari
  - Gujarati
  - Hebrew
  - Kazakh
  - Kirghiz
  - Kurdish
  - Pashto
  - Persian (Farsi)
  - Turkish
  - Urdu
  - Uzbek
  - Other
- North & South America
  - Guarani
  - Haitian (Creole)
  - Navajo
  - Quechua
  - Spanish
  - Other
- Pacific Islands
  - Fijian

- *Hawaiian*
- *Javanese*
- *Maori*
- *Samoan*
- *Other*
- Miscellaneous
  - *ESL*
  - *Esperanto*
  - *Latin*
  - *Sign Language*
  - *Yiddish*
  - *Other*

Geography
- United States
- World

Health & Fitness
- Integrated
- First Aid
- Growth & Development
- Hygiene/Personal Care
- Nutrition
- Physical Education
- Safety/Prevention

History
- American
- World
- Anthropology/Archaeology

Home Management
- Integrated
- Automotive Upkeep
- Child Care
- Cosmetology

- Culinary Arts
- Hospitality & Tourism
- Interior Design
- Maintenance/Repair
- Metallurgy
- Textile Arts/Fashion Design
- Woodworking/Carpentry

Language Arts
- Integrated
- Composition
  - *Creative*
  - *Expository*
- Drama/Theater
- Grammar
- Literature—Texts
  - *Primary*
  - *Intermediate*
  - *Youth/Teen*
- Literary Analysis
- Penmanship
- Public Speaking
- Reading/Phonics
- Spelling
- Vocabulary

Life Skills
- Character/Manners
- Driver Education
- Personal Finance
- Speed Reading

Math
- Elementary
- Secondary

- *Integrated*
- *Algebra 1*
- *Algebra 2*
- *Calculus*
- *General Math*
- *Geometry*
- *Pre-Algebra*
- *Pre-Calculus*
- *Statistics*
- *Trigonometry*

Music
- Appreciation/History
- Composition
- Listening/Enjoyment
- Theory
- Instrumental Technique
  - *Banjo*
  - *Brass*
  - *Guitar/Bass*
  - *Hand Bells*
  - *Harmonica*
  - *Harp*
  - *Mandolin*
  - *Ocarina*
  - *Organ*
  - *Percussion*
  - *Piano*
  - *Recorder*
  - *Strings*
  - *Tin Whistle*
  - *Ukulele*
  - *Voice*
  - *Woodwinds*
  - *Other*

Religious Education
- Apologetics/Worldview
- Bible Study/Theology
- Christian Living
- Devotional
- Scripture Memory
- Sunday School/VBS
- Denomination-Specific (Christian)
- Tenet-Specific (Other-than-Christian)

Science
- Elementary
- Secondary
  - *Astronomy*
  - *Biology*
    - Integrated
    - Botany
    - Human Anatomy & Physiology
    - Microbiology
    - Zoology/Veterinary Science
  - *Chemistry*
  - *Earth Science*
  - *Forensics*
  - *General Science*
  - *History of Science*
  - *Origins*
  - *Physical Science*
  - *Physics*
  - *STEM*

Social Sciences
- Civics
- Criminal Justice

- Economics
- Logic/Critical Thinking
- Philosophy
- Psychology
- Sociology
- "Social Studies"

Special Subjects
- Academic Competitions
- Accredited Programs
- Advanced Placement (AP)
- Dual Enrollment
- MOOCs

Technology
- AutoCAD/Engineering
- Coding/Computer Programming
- Drafting/Architecture
- Electronics/Robotics
- Game Design
- Web Design

Academic Support
- Brain Training
- Career Exploration
- Research Tools
- Standardized Test Prep
- Study Skills
- Tutoring

Community-Based Youth Organizations

Educational Games & Toys
- Activity Books

- Board/Card Games
- Digital Games
- Puzzles
- Subscription Boxes
- Toys

Educational Media
- Magazines
- Audio Libraries
- Video Libraries

Worksheets/Printables

Special Needs
- ADD/ADHD
- Autism/Aspergers/PDD
- Cerebral Palsy (CP)
- Cognitive Disabilities
  - *Down Syndrome*
  - *Dyscalculia*
  - *Dysgraphia*
  - *Dyslexia*
  - *Fetal Alcohol Syndrome (FAS)*
  - *Learning Disabilities (LD)*
  - *Traumatic Brain Injury (TBI)*
- Emotional Disturbance (ED)
- Epilepsy/Seizure Disorders
- Gifted & Talented
- Right-Brain Learners
- Sensory Disorders
  - *Auditory/Sensory Processing*
  - *Hearing Impairment/Deafness*
  - *Visual Impairment/Blindness*
- Speech & Language

AGES 0-5

MULTI-SUBJECT PACKAGES

- Charlotte Mason/Living Books
- Classical
- Guided Unschooling
- Montessori/Reggio/Waldorf
- Principle Approach
- Thomas Jefferson Education
- Project-Based Learning
- Traditional/School-Style
- Unit Studies

INDIVIDUAL SUBJECTS

Art

Bible

Character/Manners

Community-Based Youth Orgs

Culinary Arts

Educational Games & Toys

- Activity Books
- Board/Card Games
- Digital Games
- Puzzles
- Subscription Boxes
- Toys

Educational Media

- Magazines
- Audio Libraries
- Video Libraries

Foreign Language

- Africa
- Asia
  - *Bengali*
  - *Chinese*
  - *Hindi*
  - *Japanese*
  - *Korean*
  - *Tagalog (Filipino)*
  - *Thai*
  - *Vietnamese*
  - *Other*
- Europe
  - *Bulgarian*
  - *Croatian*
  - *Czech*
  - *Danish*
  - *Dutch*
  - *Finnish*
  - *French*
  - *German*
  - *Greek*
  - *Hungarian*
  - *Italian*
  - *Norwegian*
  - *Polish*
  - *Portuguese*
  - *Romanian*
  - *Russian*
  - *Slovak*
  - *Swedish*
  - *Other*

- Middle East
  - *Arabic*
  - *Hebrew*
  - *Persian (Farsi)*
  - *Turkish*
  - *Urdu*
  - *Other*
- North & South America
  - *Spanish*
  - *Other*
- Pacific Islands
- Miscellaneous
  - *ESL*
  - *Sign Language*
  - *Other*

Health & Fitness

History & Geography

Language Arts
- Integrated
- Drama/Theater
- Literature—Texts
- Penmanship
- Reading/Phonics

Math

Music
  - *Appreciation/History*
  - *Listening/Enjoyment*
  - *Instrumental Technique*

Science

"Social Studies"

Worksheets/Printables

Special Needs
- ADD/ADHD
- Autism/Aspergers/PDD
- Cerebral Palsy (CP)
- Cognitive Disabilities
  - *Down Syndrome*
  - *Fetal Alcohol Syndrome (FAS)*
  - *Traumatic Brain Injury (TBI)*
- Emotional Disturbance (ED)
- Epilepsy/Seizure Disorders
- Gifted & Talented
- Sensory Disorders
  - *Auditory/Sensory Processing*
  - *Hearing Impairment/Deafness*
  - *Visual Impairment/Blindness*
- Speech & Language

ACKNOWLEDGMENTS

I want first to thank Kathy Koch because without her book *8 Great Smarts: Discover and Nurture Your Child's Intelligences*, this book wouldn't exist! More than that, though, I thank her for believing in and supporting me—as a writer, homeschooler, and mom—through all the years we've been friends.

I also thank Jerry Price and Craig Abrams, whose wise, godly counsel helped me navigate through the effects of some difficult life circumstances and enabled me to grow and mature despite myself. I regret that Jerry isn't here to read this book, but I trust he somehow knows about it from his vantage point in heaven. I'm grateful to pastors David George, Jonathan Peters, and Paul Garrison for solidly preaching the Word through my infant and adolescent years in the faith, and for my good friends—especially

Lynn Gregory but others as well—who have pilgrimed with me over the years.

I appreciate the support I've enjoyed from my family—Tom and Melisa Gmirek and nephew Sam—and my husband's family—Gerald and Geraldine Hollenbeck, Nancy Hollenbeck, Chris and Kristy Hollenbeck, Eric and Patty Hollenbeck, nieces Jordyn, Sinclair, Olivia, and Annaliese, and nephews Max and Brady. I know I've sometimes seemed "weird" to them—but they've loved me anyway.

I'm blessed to have been part of a wonderful homeschool organization—the Green Bay Area Christian Homeschoolers (GBACH)—since my girls were toddlers. Whether they knew it or not, veterans in that group—Wendy Jung, Vivian Lawyer, Paula Moran, Rehna Bernhardt, to name just a few—served as my early role models. God also gave my whole family our "tribe" through the GBACH activities and events in which we participated. And I met some of my dearest friends—fellow homeschool travelers Denise Wadzinski, Julie Schroeder, Renee Janssen, Karen Schumacher, and Janet Lemke, among others—through GBACH as well.

In addition, I'm fortunate to have learned from modern homeschool pioneers like Susan Schaeffer Macaulay, Carole Joy Seid, and Barbara Shelton, and to count other pioneers—Julie Agen, Chris Wilke, Bobbie Howard, and Karen Campbell— among my personal friends. And, through various online groups over the years, I've benefitted from the wisdom, support, and friendship of other fellow homeschooling parents, including (but not limited to) Nikki Warren, Emma Brohard, Carla Baker, Amy Tennant, Robert Burley, Norine Moss, and Gail Nelson.

Thanks go as well to those who have allowed me to share snippets of their lives in these pages, to those who read and reviewed my manuscript, and to John Hinkley and his team at Moody Publishers for everything they have done to bring these words from concept to completion.

Finally, I thank my husband, Jeff, who has stuck by me through thick and thin for more than thirty-five years (and counting), supported me through the development of The Roadmap and the writing of this book, and trusted me as our daughters' primary educator. I'm also grateful for the newest member of our family, our son-in-law, Gabriel, who swept Abbie off her feet and has already demonstrated that he is God's answer to my prayers for a godly husband for her.

And then to Rachel and Abbie: my gratitude runs to the depth of my soul. Without them, I'd have missed out on the privilege of mothering and the joy of homeschooling. Though God obviously first shows us His love through Jesus, He has also done so for me through my precious daughters—via their trust in and unconditional love for me. I cherish my memories of their childhood, treasure the unique relationship I have with each of them, and—though they grew up far more quickly than I'd have preferred—look forward with anticipation to how our mother-daughter bond will grow through their adult years.

Ultimately, of course, I'm indebted to the Lord—for pursuing me until I understood who Jesus is, for enabling and empowering me to grow and mature spiritually, for blessing me with my children, and for giving me these words. May "the words of my mouth and the meditation of my heart be acceptable in your sight, O LORD, my rock and my redeemer" (Ps. 19:14).

NOTES

Chapter 1: From Where Did I Come, and Where Are We Going?

1. Kathy Koch, *Five to Thrive: How to Determine If Your Core Needs Are Being Met (and What to Do When They're Not)* (Chicago: Moody Publishers, 2020); Kathy Koch, *8 Great Smarts: Discover and Nurture Your Child's Intelligences* (Chicago: Moody Publishers, 2016).

2. On the biblical basis for the decision to homeschool: R. C. Sproul Jr., *When You Rise Up: A Covenantal Approach to Homeschooling* (Phillipsburg, NJ: P&R Publishing, 2004), and Israel Wayne, *Education: Does God Have an Opinion?* (Green Forest, AR: Master Books, 2017).

3. Kathy Koch, *8 Great Smarts: Discover and Nurture Your Child's Intelligences* (Chicago: Moody Publishers, 2016), 21–23. Kathy describes ways the smarts are awakened and activated. You'll discover supportive examples throughout the book.

4. Ibid., 42–51. Kathy addresses the idea that smarts can be paralyzed and offers examples throughout the book.

5. See Jill Savage, *No More Perfect Moms: Learn to Love Your Real Life* (Chicago: Moody Publishers, 2013), and Jill Savage and Kathy Koch, *No More Perfect Kids: Love Your Kids for Who They Are* (Chicago: Moody Publishers, 2014).

6. Koch, *8 Great Smarts.* Kathy provides ideas and illustrations relevant to children's academic growth and goes on to include ways the smarts influence character, obedience, relationships, hobbies, careers, and spiritual growth.

7. The Homeschool Resource Roadmap, https://www.homeschoolroadmap.org.

8. "The Homeschool Curriculum Route-Finder Tool," The Homeschool Resource Road-map,https://www.homeschoolroadmap.org/p/the-homeschool-curriculum-route-finder.html.

9. The Roadmap can be used in several different ways to learn about homeschool material. For example, the home page (https://www.homeschoolroadmap.org) has a link to an alphabetized list—complete with links back to every company website—of all the providers I've researched. The Common Core Project (https://www.homeschoolroadmap.org/p/common-core-project.html) expands that listing to indicate each provider's position on select educational standards (i.e., the Common Core State Standards and other initiatives that have grown from Common Core). And the Deluxe Charts Project (https://www.homeschoolroadmap.org/p/deluxe-charts.html) goes further, providing a comprehensive overview—in an easy-to-read chart format—of what every provider offers, divided first by subject area and then detailing other pertinent information.

Chapter 2: Math

1. Just like many other parents and teens, homeschoolers regularly stress about meeting the math requirements for college admissions. And, unfortunately, four-year colleges routinely require four credits of "higher math" for freshmen admissions, even when a young person's planned course of study will never require mastery of such content. So, when a teen works really hard but simply isn't wired for trigonometry and calculus, such a requirement can feel like an insurmountable obstacle. But there are alternatives. First, though going right from high school to a four-year college is a cultural norm, it's not always the best course of action, even for the most academically gifted kids. In many cases, a two-year degree or an apprenticeship will fit the bill, with less angst (and debt!) because such programs do not generally have onerous admissions requirements. Second, even if the ultimate goal is a four-year degree, a family can use what I call a stepping-stone approach and begin a child's post-secondary studies at a two-year college. With an associate's degree, a community-college graduate can transfer to a four-year college, avoiding freshmen admissions requirements altogether.

2. R. Knott, "The Life and Numbers of Fibonacci," *Plus Magazine*, Millennium Mathematics Project, https://plus.maths.org/content/life-and-numbers-fibonacci.

3. Arvind Gupta, "The Interesting Connection between Math and Music," *The Vancouver Sun*, https://vancouversun.com/news/the-interesting-connection-between-math-and-music.

Chapter 3: Language Arts

1. It's reflexive to panic at the long list of topics included in "language arts." But all of these subtopics can't and shouldn't be tackled with every child every day. From a developmental perspective, there's a logical progression for introducing them. Start from infancy with reading aloud to a child every day. When a child *shows* readiness, move on to learning to read (phonics) and penmanship, and if that's all you do for some time, don't fret.

Then, when a child can confidently read CVC words (i.e., such as *cat, dog, mud,* which follow the consonant-vowel-consonant pattern), introduce spelling. Practice these three for some time, until you're confident of mastery. You'll be working on grammar, literary analysis, vocabulary, public speaking, and composition informally all along by modeling correct standard spoken grammar, reading aloud to your kids (even after they can read for themselves), talking with them about what you read, and listening as a child regales you with oral storytelling and real-life accounts of his life experiences. But there is no need to introduce any other subtopics in a formal way for a few years. As a child begins to shift from concrete to abstract thinking—often between the ages of ten and twelve—you can put phonics, penmanship, and spelling into "maintenance mode" and replace them with direct, formal instruction in grammar, written composition, and literary analysis. Some also begin formal vocabulary instruction at that time, though others continue to keep it informal, using their kids' extensive reading to naturally grow strong vocabularies. Public speaking, too, might be tackled more formally in the tween/teen years or may continue to be addressed situationally, as circumstances dictate.

2. *Pocahontas,* The Animated Hero Classics, NEST Family Entertainment, 2005.

3. Laurie J. White, *King Alfred's English: A History of the Language We Speak and Why We Should Be Glad We Do* (Covington, GA: The Shorter Word Press, 2009).

4. Marie Rippel, "The Orton-Gillingham Approach to Reading and Spelling," *All About Learning Press,* https://blog.allaboutlearningpress.com/orton-gillingham/.

5. Sonya Shafer, "How to Do Copywork," *Simply Charlotte Mason,* https://simplycharlotte mason.com/blog/how-to-do-copywork/; Sonya Shafer, "How to Do Transcription," *Simply Charlotte Mason,* https://simplycharlottemason.com/blog/how-to-do-transcription/.

6. Tina Hollenbeck, "Fostering Your Kids' Love for Literature," Views from the Road Home, August 11, 2018, https://www.viewsfromtheroadhome.org/2018/08/foster ing-your-kids-love-for-literature.html.

7. Some homeschooling parents get hung up on diagramming, elevating it as the "only" viable method of teaching grammar. Diagramming is helpful to some kids, but it's not the only option and definitely doesn't work all the time. Another method, parsing, involves labeling words in sentences without building the elaborate diagramming webs that confuse some kids; two programs that utilize parsing are *Easy Grammar* (ISHA) and *Winston Grammar* (Precious Memories). Other kids come to understand the nuances of English grammar only when they learn a second language, as they apply to English what they learn while analyzing the grammar of a new language. Still others (most likely the very word smart) seem to absorb correct standard usage as if by osmosis, simply from reading well-written literature and other texts. Diagramming is not evil, but neither should it be idealized or idolized.

8. Tina Hollenbeck, "De-Mystifying the Writing Process," Views from the Road Home, November 16, 2018, https://www.viewsfromtheroadhome.org/2018/11/de-mystify ing-writing-process.html.

9. During my classroom teaching career, I worked with tweens and teens for whom English was a second language. All of them—even the toughest high school senior guys—loved when I read aloud to them. My husband read aloud to our daughters, often choosing classics they might not have picked to read on their own, well into their high school years. Family read-aloud time has long been a hallmark among homeschoolers; be part of continuing that tradition with your kids.

10. Koch, *8 Great Smarts*, 106–107, the "close your eyes and see" technique.

11. "What Is a Mind Map?," MindMapping.com, https://www.mindmapping.com/mind-map.

12. Tina Hollenbeck, "The Art of Buddy-Reading," Views from the Road Home, August 27, 2020, https://www.viewsfromtheroadhome.org/2020/08/the-art-of-buddy-reading.html.

Chapter 4: Science

1. Pam Barnhill, "Loop Scheduling vs. Block Scheduling: Which Is Right for Your Homeschool?," Your Morning Basket, https://pambarnhill.com/loop-scheduling/.

2. Sonya Shafer, "8 Great Reasons to Do Nature Study," *Simply Charlotte Mason*, https://simplycharlottemason.com/blog/8-reasons-to-do-nature-study/.

3. *STEM* is an acronym for Science, Technology, Engineering, and Mathematics. A similar acronym is *STEAM,* which incorporates Art as well. Both approaches are characterized by the use of inquiry-based, hands-on learning. A synonymous phrase is "applied science."

4. Koch, *8 Great Smarts*, 208.

5. Jamie Erickson, "What Is a Living Book Anyway?" *The Unlikely Homeschool*, https://www.theunlikelyhomeschool.com/2019/11/living-book.html.

6. Opinions vary about the merits of the Common Core State Standards (CCSS), Next Generation Science Standards (NGSS), and similar initiatives, which were initially designed, beginning in 2009, for use in American public schools. Though not mandated for homeschoolers in any state, some homeschool resources began adopting these standards in 2013, as described in the Common Core Project section of The Homeschool Resource Roadmap (https://www.homeschoolroadmap.org/p/common-core-project.html). I dug into the content and goals of the standards and determined for a number of reasons (https://www.viewsfromtheroadhome.org/2018/08/common-core-whats-big-deal.html) to avoid them with my girls. Because these standards are incorporated into some (but not the majority of) homeschool resources, take time to research them for yourself in order to make an intentional decision about whether to incorporate them into your home-education program.

7. Koch, *8 Great Smarts,* 153.

Chapter 5: Social Studies

1. Alt: WI—Embracing Homeschool Freedom in Wisconsin, https://www.facebook.com/groups/altwi.

2. The Roadmap's Deluxe Charts Project includes lists of educational games and toys for all ages, many related to various academic subject areas (https://www.homeschoolroadmap.org/p/deluxe-charts-ages-5-18.html).

3. "Homeschool Philosophies Quiz," Eclectic Homeschooling, http://eclectic-homeschool .com/homeschool-philosophies-quiz/. Eclectic Homeschooling labels the homeschool learning styles as Charlotte Mason, Classical Education, Montessori Education, Project-Based Learning, Reggio-Inspired, Thomas Jefferson Education, Traditional Education, Unit Studies Approach, Unschooling Approach, and Waldorf Education. Within The Homeschool Resource Roadmap, I utilize similar labels and have added the Principle Approach, Roadschooling, and Tutorial.

4. In practical terms, homeschool curricula often differentiate between America and the rest of the world (that is, distinct resources exist for American History and United States Geography, separate from World History and World Geography). Current high school social studies electives usually include psychology, sociology, and (sometimes) criminology and anthropology/archaeology. Because the "Humanities" label is no longer commonly used in K–12 education, The Homeschool Resource Roadmap also lists logic/critical thinking and philosophy under its social studies headers.

5. Our 2008 tour began in Pepin, Wisconsin, where Laura Ingalls was born. After a short detour to Burr Oak, Iowa, we traveled all the way across Minnesota—through Mankato and Sleepy Eye to Walnut Grove and the Ingalls' real homestead on the banks of Plum Creek—and into De Smet, South Dakota, where we toured Ingalls-related buildings in town and spent an entire day out on their homestead property. In 2014, we headed for Williamsburg, Virginia (by way, because it was relatively en route, of the Creation Museum in Kentucky), then wound our way north to Mount Vernon and Gettysburg, Pennsylvania. My husband has done mission work in Trinidad for years, under the auspices of his ministry, MissionGuides (www.missionguides.org). He was thrilled to show Trini culture to our girls and their friends.

6. "Field Trip Venues," The Homeschool Resource Roadmap, https://www.homeschool roadmap.org/p/field-trip-venues.html. The Roadmap lists extensive field trip ideas for every Canadian province and U.S. state.

Chapter 6: Fine Arts

1. Koch, *8 Great Smarts*, 97, 141–143.

2. Ibid., 59, 79.

3. John Taylor Gatto, *The Underground History of American Education: A School Teacher's Intimate Investigation into the Problem of Modern Schooling* (New York: The Oxford Village Press, 2000); John Holt, *How Children Fail* (Pitman, 1964; Delacorte, 1982; Perseus, 1995); Raymond S. Moore and Dorothy N. Moore, *Better Late Than Early: A New Approach to Your Child's Education* (Camas, WA: The Moore Foundation, 1975).

4. Barry Stebbing, owner of *How Great Thou Art*, no longer travels, but other artists do.

Chapter 7: Electives

1. Homeschool law varies from state to state. Some states delineate a few general high school graduation requirements for homeschoolers, but none demand that homeschoolers mimic the mandates set for public school graduation. To that end, I urge you to ignore

public school graduation regulations and base high-school planning for your children on two things: the actual language of the *homeschool* law in your state of residence and what each child may actually need in order to pursue his next step in life. For example, if the goal is immediate enrollment in a four-year college, study the admissions requirements spelled out on college websites and build a high-school study program based on those requirements, not what any public (or even private) school requires of its students. If a teen is planning to attend a two-year college or trade school, enlist in the military, or move immediately to the work world, adjust accordingly. Never use public school requirements as a default; as a homeschooler, you are independent of the public-school system. As long as you can demonstrate that you've complied with your state's homeschool law and your child has met the admission requirements for his desired next step, he won't be hindered in moving forward. Many colleges actively recruit homeschoolers precisely because their high school studies have been uniquely customized.

2. Tina Hollenbeck, "Homeschool 'Graduation Requirements,'" Views from the Road Home, December 1, 2020, https://www.viewsfromtheroadhome.org/2020/12/homeschool-graduation-requirements.html. Homeschooling parents often fret over how to award high school credit, but it's not nearly as complicated as it might seem.

Chapter 8: Religious Education

1. "What Is a Worldview?—Definition & Introduction," American Scientific Affiliation, https://asa3.org/ASA/education/views/index.html.

2. Elsie Egermeier, *Egermeier's Bible Story Book* (Anderson, IN: The Warner Press, 1927); Catherine F. Vos, *The Child's Story Bible* (Grand Rapids, MI: Wm. B. Eerdmans Publishing Co., 1934).

3. Koch, *8 Great Smarts*, 69–70, 91–93, 114–17, 135–37, 159–60, 181–82, 200–202, and 218–19.

Chapter 9: The Bottom Line

1. At the time of this book's publication, *The Homeschool Resource Roadmap* lists, links to, and categorizes more than 4,900 educational resource providers. I regularly add to and update the listings.

2. Bobbie Howard, *Encouragement Along the Way: A Devotional Guide & Journal for Home Schooling Parents* (Gresham, OR: Noble Publishing Associates, 1993).

3. Karen Campbell, *The Joy of Relationship Homeschooling: When the One Anothers Come Home* (Canton, IL: Karen Campbell, 2014).

4. The Mom Psychologist, http://www.themompsychologist.com/.

ABOUT THE AUTHOR

As a teen, Tina Hollenbeck called herself an atheist and knew beyond a shadow of a doubt that she'd become a veterinarian. She was also certain that, though she'd probably eventually have children, she might not bother with marriage. Instead—and much to her surprise!—God revealed Himself to her when she was a college freshman, and He transformed the trajectory of her life. She married her husband, Jeff, when she was just twenty-one and changed her college major several times before eventually graduating *magna cum laude* with a bachelor's in humanities. All of this goes to show that God definitely redirects our paths despite our plans (Prov. 16:9) and that He has a sense of humor!

Tina worked for a short time as her church's secretary before returning to college to pursue teacher certification, after which she spent nine years helping immigrant kids in public schools to learn English. Though she and Jeff lost their first daughter, Anna Vivian, to miscarriage, Tina "transferred" to homeschooling the moment Rachel was born and never looked back. She now advocates for and writes about various topics related to homeschooling and healthy parenting.

In 2013, Tina began a research project culminating in the development of The Homeschool Resource Roadmap, a free database that provides useful information about virtually every learning resource available to homeschoolers. The Roadmap's extensive lists and charts enable parents to make wise, well-informed decisions as they seek to provide a customized education for each of their children.

Tina has served since 2006 as a volunteer writer for Celebrate Kids, a ministry that "renews and revitalizes parents and their children so they value their family unit and are known there, wanted there, and able to establish strong, rooted relationships." Tina writes for the ministry's blog and coauthored a booklet entitled *Celebrating Children's 12 Genius Qualities* (Celebrate Kids, 2014).

When she was just ten years old—even before hatching her grand plan to become a veterinarian—Tina wrote an illustrated children's book about a family of dogs. From that point on, she kept the dream of one day becoming "a real published author" in the back of her mind. Now, despite all the other ways the Lord has redirected her youthful desires, He has brought that aspiration to fruition with the publication of *8 Great Smarts for Homeschoolers.*

In her spare time, Tina engages her music smart by singing on her church's worship team, activates her body smart by exercising, mobilizes her picture smart by scrapbooking, and stimulates her people smart via coffee dates with old and new friends.

CELEBRATE KIDS

Founded in 1991 by Dr. Kathy Koch, Celebrate Kids partners with parents to strengthen family relationships and develop children's unique God-given gifts and talents so they can live on purpose with intentionality.

In the words of Dr. Kathy, "We are all created on purpose, with purpose, and for purpose." This simple statement defines the ministry objectives as we especially help people understand the following:

We are all intentionally created by a heavenly Father who loves us and wants His best for us.

We are purposefully created to serve Him through our interests, strengths, and even our challenges. God makes no mistakes!

Parents need to be strong and help children live long so they can hear and see God direct their steps in the present and for the future. We all have reasons to be here!

Celebrate Kids teams with parents and children to help them realize their unique gifts and talents through books, speaking, conferences, social media, blogs, podcasts, online courses, and more so they can live their lives intentionally in gratitude to their Creator.

In 2020, after almost 30 years in ministry, Dr. Kathy, her board of directors, and her staff knew that changes were coming. Celebrate Kids acquired Ignite the Family as our conference ministry to disciple the whole family to a deeper relationship with Christ. Through our signature women's event, Ignite Women's Conference, and other strategic offerings for married couples, parents, grandparents, men, and children, Celebrate Kids is poised to change the landscape of how we relate to each other.

Celebrate Kids and Dr. Kathy have been blessed to partner with Moody Publishers, Focus on the Family, Care Net, The Colson Center, Summit Ministries, Teach Them Diligently, ACSI, UMSI, AXIS, and several other nationally recognized ministries.

To get more information about Celebrate Kids, or to find out how you can get involved with the ministry, go to celebratekids.com or find us on social media. Celebrate Kids, Inc., is a 501(c)(3) non-profit ministry.

DON'T JUST CHANGE WHAT YOUR CHILDREN DO.
CHANGE WHAT THEY *BELIEVE*.